RUN with the WINNERS

BOOKS BY WARREN W. WIERSBE

RUN with the WINNERS

*Developing a Championship
Lifestyle from Hebrews 11*

Warren W. Wiersbe

kregel
PUBLICATIONS

Grand Rapids, MI 49501

Run with the Winners: Developing a Championship Lifestyle from Hebrews 11 by Warren W. Wiersbe.

Copyright © 1985 by Warren W. Wiersbe.

Published in 1995 by Kregel Publications, a division of Kregel, Inc., P. O. Box 2607, Grand Rapids, MI 49501. Kregel Publications provides trusted, biblical publications for Christian growth and service. Your comments and suggestions are valued.

Unless otherwise stated, all Scripture quotations are from the *New American Standard Bible*, © 1960, 1962, 1963, 1968, 1971 by The Lockman Foundation, La Habra, California.

Cover Photograph: Photodisc
Cover Design: Alan G. Hartman

Library of Congress Cataloging-in-Publication Data
Wiersbe, Warren W.
Run with the winners: developing a championship lifestyle from Hebrews 11 / Warren W. Wiersbe.
    p. cm.
    Originally published: Wheaton, Ill.: Tyndale House, 1985.
    1. Bible. N.T. Hebrews XI—Criticism, interpretation, etc.
2. Faith—Biblical teaching. I. Title.
BS2775.2.W52   1995   227'.8706—dc20   94-37815
                                        CIP

ISBN 0-8254-3997-3 (paperback)

1 2 3 4 5 Printing / Year 99 98 97 96 95

Printed in the United States of America

Dedicated to the best neighbors
anybody could ever want:
Bob and Idonna Florell,
Brenda, David, and especially Scott

CONTENTS

PREFACE

I'm the last person in the world who ought to be writing about anything that relates to athletics! But if I avoided all the athletic references in the Bible, I would be depriving myself of the kind of spiritual encouragement that all of us need in these difficult days.

Hebrews 11 is about the winners—ordinary people who discovered that the secret of staying on top is not talent, opportunities, or status: it's faith in God. These people were not perfect. They failed often. Some of them got on painful detours and had to be disciplined by God. But all of them reached their goal successfully and accomplished what God wanted them to do.

These studies are based on a series of messages originally given at The Moody Church in Chicago when I was serving there as senior minister. In a revised form, they were given over Back to the Bible Broadcast, where I now serve as associate teacher. I trust that these studies will be a help to God's people as they run the race of faith.

"And this is the victory that has overcome the world— our faith" (1 John 5:4).

Warren W. Wiersbe

1/ FOCUS ON FAITH
HEBREWS 11:1–3, 6

Whenever I hear somebody call Hebrews 11 "The
Westminster Abbey of Faith," I cringe inside. My wife
and I have often visited the Abbey, and, quite frankly, I
don't see how Hebrews 11 has much in common with
that historic landmark.

For one thing, the Abbey is a museum and a cemetery,
while Hebrews 11 throbs with excitement and life. Most
of the people honored in Westminster Abbey were also
honored during their lifetimes, while the people listed in
Hebrews 11 were looked upon as radicals, rebels, and
troublemakers.

As I have walked about Westminster Abbey, I have seen
the names of gifted people, many of them geniuses in
their field. But, for the most part, the people named in
Hebrews 11 were ordinary "garden variety" people who
accomplished great things. Gideon was a frightened
farmer when God called him. Moses was a fugitive from
justice. Jephthah was an illegitimate son, unwanted by
his family.

The people enshrined in Westminster Abbey are there
because they did great things. The people named in

Hebrews 11 are there because they *could not do great things*, so they trusted God to do great things for them. The Hebrews 11 heroes were distinguished, not by their names or titles, but by their faith. They all trusted God and God used them to change the world.

I prefer to call Hebrews 11 "God's Hall of Fame of Faith." Why? Because the entire context of this chapter is athletic. The climax of the chapter is not 11:40 but 12:1-3, and there the emphasis is on *running the race*. Hebrews 11 presents these men and women of faith as dedicated athletes who reached their goal and won their prize because they had faith in God and obeyed the rules of the game. *They were not quitters!*

The believers to whom the book of Hebrews was written needed this kind of message. They were experiencing opposition and persecution (10:32-39) and were in danger of giving up the race and turning back. Some of the members of the fellowship had been arrested and put into prison (13:3), and others were having to bear reproach as Christians (13:13). "Let us press on to maturity!" is the clarion call of the book (6:1). "Let us run with endurance the race that is set before us" (12:1).

Do we need this kind of message today? We certainly do! As we run our race of faith, we face the same obstacles and distractions that the patriarchs and prophets faced. Tough times demand tough faith; and the more we trust God, the stronger our "faith muscles" become. When young Jeremiah was about to drop out of the race, God said to him: "If you have run with the footmen and they have tired you out, then how can you compete with horses? If you fall down in a land of peace, how will you do in the thicket of the Jordan?" (Jeremiah 12:5).

If you and I are going to win the race and reach the goals God has set for us, we must understand what it means to live by faith. To help us understand, the writer introduces this exciting chapter by answering four fundamental questions.

1. WHAT IS BIBLE FAITH?

It never ceases to amaze and disturb me, the way many people define *faith*. "Things are going to work out—I have faith!" says one person, practicing blind optimism. "Why, yes, I have faith that the Bible is true," says another. "I'm not worried!" states a third person. "Faith always works!" Try to tell him that he has *faith in faith*, instead of faith in God, and he will argue with you.

The usual definition of faith is that it is "believing in spite of evidence," and no definition could be farther from the truth. To believe in spite of evidence is really superstition, not faith; because *faith is only as good as the object*. If you have faith in your doctor, you will get what your doctor can give you. If you have faith in God, you will get what God can give you.

What kind of faith did the "runners" in Hebrews 11 have? *It was faith that acted.* It was not just mental assent (intellectual faith) or emotional concern (faith in faith); it involved obedience to God's Word. Note the verbs given in Hebrews 11: Abel *offered* a sacrifice; Noah *prepared* an ark; Abraham *offered up* Isaac; Moses *left* Egypt; and so on. If we are going to run the race of faith, we have to *do* something. We cannot run and stand still at the same time!

According to the Bible, true faith is *obeying God in spite of feelings, circumstances, or consequences.* All of the men and women whose names are listed in "The Hall of Fame of Faith" had to deal with their emotions (did you ever walk through a sea?), their circumstances (did you ever fight an army?), and the consequences of their decisions (did you ever say no to a powerful ruler?). They did not deny their feelings; they could not change their circumstances; they could not predict the consequences. *But they trusted God*, and He saw them through.

The object of faith is God. Everybody has faith in something—a job, money, friends, a political party, you name it. The difference between the Christian and the non-Christian is not that one has faith and the other doesn't. The difference is that the Christian has faith *in God*. It is the *object* of faith that makes the believer's faith real and powerful.

The sphere of faith is the invisible and the impossible. Dr. J. Oswald Sanders has stated it perfectly: "Faith enables the believing soul to treat the future as present and the invisible as seen." Abraham left an earthly city because he saw, by faith, a heavenly city (11:10). Moses forsook Egypt because he saw a greater inheritance for his people. The presence of faith in the heart is the assurance that we will receive what has been promised. No matter what the circumstances around us may be, faith gives us *the assurance* that God will prevail. No matter what the consequences before us, faith gives us *the conviction* that God will triumph. Faith gives us eyes to see and feet to stand on when everything around us threatens us, and everything ahead of us looks like disaster.

In other words, true Bible faith has to do with the *inner person*, not the outer circumstances. With the "eyes of the heart" we see the invisible. With the "ears of the heart" we hear God speak to us through His Word. We see the invisible, hear the inaudible, touch the intangible, and do the impossible!

If all of this sounds "mystical" to you, let me remind you that *this is the way all creative people function*. Artists, composers, writers, even scientists, pay close attention to the inner person. Max Planck, the man who discovered the quantum theory, says that the scientist who wants to pioneer new territory must realize that "new ideas are not generated by deduction, but by *artistically* creative imagination." The scientist depends as much on intuition and "educated hunches" as he does experiments and statistics.

So, if you and I are going to be among the winners in the race of faith, we must learn how to develop this amazing inner faculty that is called faith. This leads us to the second question.

2. HOW DOES BIBLE FAITH WORK?
There are at least four steps involved in the exercise of true Bible faith.

(a) *Revelation—the Word of God.* The God we know is the God who speaks. "God, after He spoke long ago to the fathers . . . in these last days has spoken to us in His Son . . ." (Hebrews 1:1, 2). The basic theme of Hebrews is "God has spoken! What are you doing about it?" The fact that we have a Bible is a serious thing. "See to it that you do not refuse Him who is speaking" (Hebrews 12:25).

We dare not separate faith from the Word of God. "So faith comes from hearing, and hearing by the word of Christ" (Romans 10:17). In one way or another, God communicated His truth to all of the people named in Hebrews 11. Their faith was generated by, and founded on, the revealed Word of God. Moses was not afraid of the Egyptian army because God had told him that He would safely deliver the Jews from Egypt. Joshua was not embarrassed to march around Jericho for a week, because God had told him he would conquer the city.

Granted, God doesn't speak to us today in exactly the same way He spoke to Moses and Joshua; *and I'm glad He doesn't.* If I were to hear voices, or see visions, I might wonder if they came from God or Satan. Or, it's possible that I might misunderstand what was said. You and I have something surer: a complete and final revelation from God in Jesus Christ, recorded in the Word. If we know the God of the Word, through faith in Jesus Christ, then we can know the Word of God and understand what it is God wants us to do.

How do we do this?

(b) *Relationship—a walk with God.* The winners in the race of faith were people who maintained a relationship with God, one that deepened with each step of faith. Too many people today (including Christian people) ignore God day after day, and then run to Him when a crisis occurs. All of a sudden, they want Him to give them the faith they need to fight the war or solve the problem. When they don't get what they want, they get angry with God and tell everybody that faith doesn't work.

Well, if they applied that same approach to any other area of life, they would fail just as miserably. Imagine what would happen to an athlete who didn't spend time with his coach! Do you think he'd ever make it to the Olympics? The musician must build a creative relationship with his teacher if he or she ever hopes to make it to Carnegie Hall.

Hebrews 11:6 spells this out. To begin with, the purpose of the life of faith is *to please God.* It is not to become famous, or even to accomplish great things for God. Our purpose is to *please* God. Everything in the life of faith is a by-product of our desire to please the Father. Otherwise, faith can become a "tool" whereby we "use God" to accomplish the things that we want to do. When I hear people talking about "exercising faith" in order to receive healing, better jobs, more money, and "real success," I wonder if they know that the basic purpose for faith is to please God, to glorify God.

If we want to please God, we will *come to God.* This means fellowship, spending time in worship and communion. Abel was found at the altar. Enoch walked with God. Even when a lad, Samuel heard God speak. The better you get to know your friends, the easier it is to trust them—or *not* trust them, as the case may be. Evangelist D. L. Moody said, "I used to think I should close my Bible and pray for faith; but I came to see that it was in studying the Word that I was to get faith." As we come to

God and His Word, we develop a relationship that
deepens day by day.

Hebrews 11:6 indicates that this relationship involves
not only pleasing God and coming to God, but also
seeking God. This implies a deep desire to know Him
better and to please Him more. "Let the heart of those
who seek the Lord be glad. Seek the Lord and His
strength; seek His face continually" (Psalm 105:3, 4). The
masters of the devotional life have reminded us that God
is the *source* of our spiritual yearnings, the *strength* of
them, and their *goal.* We seek the Lord because He first
seeks us. It is an assuring truth that the Father is *seeking*
people to worship Him (John 4:23). And when we find
Him, we discover that the quest begins all over again!

(c) *Response—doing the will of God.* Faith is not a
feeling, although it certainly involves the emotions. Faith
is more than assent to facts written in a book, although
we dare not bypass our intellect as we relate to God. True
faith involves the will: we act upon God's Word. Faith is
obeying God, in spite of feelings, circumstances, or
consequences. Abraham's neighbors thought he was
crazy; yet at age seventy-five he took his wife and headed
for an unknown land. As Halford Luccock put it, he
marched right off the map! "By faith Abraham, when he
was called, obeyed by going out . . ." (11:8).

If we are practicing true Bible faith, there will be a total
response on our part. The mind will know God's will; the
emotions will desire to do God's will; and the will itself
will respond and obey God's call. I suppose we can call
this threefold response perception (the mind), persuasion
(the emotions), and performance (the will).

When we study the lives of the great men and women
of faith, we discover that often, when they obeyed God,
everything seemed to go wrong! Abraham arrived in the
Promised Land only to walk into a famine. Moses and

Aaron confronted Pharaoh only to be driven out and then
to have their own people turn against them. Israel de-
parted from Egypt, only to face an impassable sea and be
followed by an angry army. If you have the idea that the
life of faith means smooth seas and easy roads, you are in
for a shock.

What was it, then, that kept these people running the
race?

(d) *Reward—the witness of God.* God is "a rewarder of
those who seek Him" (11:6). He keeps His promises and
fulfills His purposes. And He keeps us going by putting
His witness in our hearts that we are doing His will.

One of the key words in Hebrews 11 is *witness.* It is
translated "gained approval" in verse 2, "obtained the
testimony" in verse 4, "obtained the witness" in verse 5,
and "gained approval" in verse 39—but it is the same
Greek word. When we exercise faith in God, we receive
the inner witness from God; and this witness keeps us
going when the going is tough. The Word of God is the
objective side of faith, and the witness of God is the
subjective side of faith. We need both if we are going to be
winners.

If we divorce these two factors, we may end up in one
of two dangerous extremes. If all we have is the objective
witness of the Bible, we may have a mere intellectual
faith; or we may be applying to ourselves some promise
that doesn't really belong to us. I have a friend who
claimed John 11:4 ("This sickness is not unto death . . .")
for a loved one, but the person died anyway. The verse
was true, but she didn't have that inner witness from God
that *she* should claim it in this case.

On the other hand, we usually go to the *subjective*
extreme: we have a "feeling" down inside that God is
about to do some great thing. We can't document this
"feeling" from the Bible, but we accept it anyway and act
upon it. *Beware of spiritual feelings that can't be sup-*

ported by scriptural facts. A friend of mine was "sure" God wanted him in Christian service, so he quit his job and made himself available. Nothing happened, and he almost went broke. Finally, he had to go back to his employer (to whom he had preached a sermon on faith) and beg for another job. A pastor I know had a "confident feeling" that God was leading the church into a building program—and the church is still trying to climb out of its chasm of debt.

All four of these factors are necessary for the life of faith. We must have the *revelation* from God's Word, the promise that He wants us to claim. This revelation comes as the result of a growing *relationship*, a day-by-day walk with God. Our *response* is to understand His will, delight in it, and act upon it; and His *reward* is to give us the inner witness that He is in control and all will turn out just as He promised. The world would look at these winners and say, "They act a bit crazy, but they sure have self-confidence!" But it was not self-confidence; it was the inner witness of God in their hearts.

In Hebrews 12:1, these winners are called "so great a cloud of witnesses." This doesn't suggest that they are watching us today, like so many spectators in a stadium. Rather, it means that they are *bearing witness* to us today. God first witnessed to them, and now they witness to us!

No matter what problem or challenge we might face, there is somebody in God's "Hall of Fame of Faith" who can encourage us. Are you moving to a different city and leaving friends and family behind? Think of Abraham; he knew what it was like to pack up and move—and he didn't know where he was going! Are you praying about a husband or wife? Think of Isaac; he had to trust God to find him a mate. Have you caused a family problem and you're afraid to face it? Spend some time with Jacob; he infuriated his brother Esau and, years later, had to face up to the consequences. Are you having to put up with economic distress or constant physical pain? The heroes of faith can identify with you and encourage you.

This, by the way, is why we have the Old Testament, among other reasons. In the Old Testament, God calls his witnesses to encourage you in the battles of life. "For whatever was written in earlier times was written for our instruction, that through perseverance and the encouragement of the Scriptures we might have hope" (Romans 15:4).

3. HOW DOES BIBLE FAITH GROW?

The Bible reveals that there are degrees of faith: no faith, little faith, faith, and great faith. When Jesus compared faith to a tiny grain of mustard seed, He wasn't speaking only of size; He also was referring to life and potential. *There is life in even the smallest seed.* A living faith in a living God, based on the living Word, has the potential for growth.

It is interesting that the first "by faith" statement in Hebrews 11 concerns the world around us. "By faith we understand that the worlds were prepared by the word of God, so that what is seen was not made out of things which are visible" (11:3). While it is important that we keep our eyes on what God says in the Word, it is also important that we keep our eyes on what God does *in His world.* When He was ministering on earth, our Lord repeatedly pointed to the works of God in nature: the Father's care for the birds and the lilies, His control of the weather, His laws that enable seeds to grow and people to be fed.

The world around us was created by the Word of God. "For He commanded and they were created" (Psalm 148:5). The world is sustained by the Word of God (2 Peter 3:5-7). Is there any reason why our lives cannot be governed by that same Word? When we live by faith, we are energized and enlightened by the same Word that runs the universe! This means that everything in God's universe will work *for* us, in spite of difficulties, tears, and seeming tragedies.

Faith grows, then, as we see God at work in His world. This does not mean we are walking by sight. Rather, it means that we are interpreting what we see in God's world by what we learn in God's Word. Abraham walked by faith and stayed out of Sodom. Lot walked by sight and moved into Sodom—and lost everything (Genesis 13:18, 19). It is no accident that the Psalms often extol the work of God in nature and in human history. A proper study of God's universe can only make a person's faith grow.

Faith also grows as we get to know God better in the pages of His Word. I am afraid of what some people call "Bible study"—outlines and analyses, charts and diagrams, etc. Each of these things has its place in serious Bible study, but none of them is an end in itself. It isn't enough to know the Word of God; we must know the God of the Word. As we sing in one of our hymns:

Beyond the sacred page
I seek Thee, Lord;
My spirit pants for Thee,
Thou living Word.

In these later years, my wife has been able to travel with me in my itinerant ministry; but this was not always so. There were times when I would be away from home two or three weeks at a time, and it was during those times that I gave thanks for the telephone and the mail service! But can you picture me receiving a long letter from home and sitting down to diagram the sentences and analyze the verbs! Of course not! The first thing I would do was enjoy the loving message that was in the letter. It was not the letter so much as the loving wife behind the letter that really counted.

If we want our faith to grow, we must get to know God better. Let's not permit our Bible study to hide God's face from our hearts. We should use every dependable tool available as we mine the riches of the Bible, not forgetting to get close to the heart of God.

Finally, our faith grows as we exercise it. There's nothing profound about that, but many people miss it. The witnesses in Hebrews 11 had to endure tests *of increasing magnitude* so that their faith could develop and grow strongor. God didn't bogin with Abraham by asking him to offer a loved one on the altar. He just asked him to pack up and leave home. Abraham went from one test to another, because the "school of faith" requires increasingly difficult examinations. Jesus didn't begin with Peter by asking him to walk on the water. Instead, He asked him to move his boat out into the deep water. God starts with the easier lessons, and then the course gets harder.

We cannot strengthen our "faith muscles" by reading a book (even the Bible) or hearing a lecture. *We have to act on what God tells us.* Faith without action is dead faith (James 2:14-26), and dead faith cannot grow. We begin the Christian life by trusting Christ to save us. Then we grow in faith and trust Him to keep us and protect us. As we grow still more, we trust Him to provide for us and to guide us. Our faith increases and strengthens as we obey God.

4. WHO CAN ENJOY THIS KIND OF FAITH?
Most of us look for some excuse to drop out of the race of faith. We see the handicaps instead of the possibilities. But the testimony of the winners will not permit us to drop out. Listen to what they say.

"Faith cleanses all kinds of sin!" In other words, our past is no handicap! All of the people whose names and exploits are listed in Hebrews 11 were, of course, sinners just like you and me. *But I dare you to find one single sin mentioned in this chapter!* Noah got drunk one day. Abraham twice lied about his wife, and his son Isaac did

the same thing. Sarah laughed at God's promise and then denied it! Moses lost his temper; David committed adultery and tried to hide his sin; Joshua "jumped the gun" and made a bad decision because he didn't ask for God's guidance. The winners didn't always collect medals; sometimes they collected scars. But not one word of their failures is recorded in Hebrews 11.

If we have trusted Jesus Christ as our Savior, then God has cleansed our sins and given us a new beginning. Our past record is not a handicap, so we must not use it as an excuse. "Well, I've always been lazy!" or "My family is known for its bad temper!" will never be accepted by God. We are a new creation in Jesus Christ, and that means new power to accomplish new victories.

"Faith changes all kinds of people!" When I read Hebrews 11, I get excited about the *variety* I see there. Here are men and women, old people and young people, kings and commoners, the high born and the illegitimate, the gifted and the ordinary; and they all have one thing in common: they dared to trust God. Moses, by faith, was transformed from an excuse-making fugitive into the great liberator and law-giver. Gideon, by faith, was transformed from a frightened farmer into a victorious general. Numerous anonymous people—all of them living by faith—were able to endure all kinds of trials and persecutions, even death, because they trusted God's Word.

Our past is no handicap and our birth is no handicap. We may conclude that we don't possess the necessary talents or abilities to serve God, but we do—by faith.

"Faith conquers all kinds of problems!" The faith life is not free of difficulties. If anything, it has more than its share of difficulties; but the difficulties are there to strengthen our faith. Enoch faced the problem of staying clean in a defiled world, and faith enabled him to do it. Noah had to stand against the ridicule of his neighbors, while Moses had to fight the opposition of the government. Daniel faced a den full of lions! And the three

Hebrew children were thrown into an inferno!

It's important to note that, while God always honors faith, He doesn't always work in the same way in all of our lives. There are times when He delivers us *from* the problems (11:32-35a), and there are times when He delivers us *in* the problems (11:35b-38). We will discuss this in detail later, but it's necessary to mention it now. Daniol was dolivorod from thc lions' den; but others, who had just as much faith, were thrown to the lions and slain. James was arrested and beheaded, while Peter was arrested and then miraculously delivered from prison (Acts 12).

If God chooses not to deliver us *from* a particular problem, we can be sure He will honor our faith and deliver us *in* that trial. Either way, He will be glorified and we will grow in our faith and in Christian character.

"Faith releases all kinds of potential!" David the shepherd boy had no idea the kind of hero God would make out of him, but faith released the potential and made it possible. The circumstances around us and the people over us cannot hinder God from achieving His purposes in and through our lives. *We have potential because we are children of God.* It is faith that will release that potential. "Be it done to you according to your faith" (Matthew 9:29).

Right now, we are living by faith; *but is it faith in God?*

We can't argue that we have no faith. *Everybody* lives by faith. If we step on an elevator, order from a menu, or take a dose of medicine, we are giving evidence of faith.

The important thing is the *object* of faith, because faith is only as good as the object.

If we have faith in God, then we can enjoy all that God can do for us.

We can start to run with the winners!

2/ ABEL:
A FAITH TO DIE FOR
GENESIS 4:1–10;
HEBREWS 11:4

Whenever people get together over a cup of coffee and discuss the problems of the world, somebody is sure to come up with a solution. The usual suggestions are:

"The problem is heredity. Some people just shouldn't have children."

"No, the real problem is environment. Unless we clean up our cities, we'll never solve the problems."

"You're both wrong! The trouble with people today is they won't work. They're lazy! It takes work to build character."

"Well, I may be wrong, but I think people need religion. If more people practiced their religion, we'd have fewer problems in this world."

Try applying these solutions to the situation of Cain and Abel. Cain was a murderer; he killed his own brother. *Heredity?* Both boys had the same parents. *Environment?* Both boys were born and raised just outside paradise. *Employment?* Both of them worked for a living, Cain as a farmer and Abel as a shepherd. *Religion?* They met at the altar, each of them with a sacrifice to present to God.

Yet Cain was a murderer! Why? Because he was an

unbeliever. The basic difference between Cain and Abel was *faith*. Cain did not really have saving faith toward God, even though he was a "religious" man. Abel's faith made a martyr out of him. Cain's unbelief made a murderer out of him.

It seems strange that the writer would start his "Hall of Fame" with a martyr. It might discourage somebody from entering the race. Why not begin with a great leader like Moses, or a popular hero like David? But the choice is a wise one: let the reader know that faith in Jesus Christ is a faith worth dying for, that running the race costs something. That will separate the runners from the spectators! "Ministry that costs nothing, accomplishes nothing," said John Henry Jowett.

Let's examine the kind of faith Abel had and discover how it can help us in our own struggles today.

1. HE HAD SAVING FAITH.

Jesus called him "righteous Abel" (Matthew 23:35), and this is echoed in Hebrews 11:4, ". . . he obtained the testimony that he was righteous." This was obviously not a self-righteousness that he had manufactured. It was a righteousness that was the gift of God in response to his faith.

Why would Abel need righteousness? After all, wasn't he the son of Adam and Eve, who were clothed by God after they had sinned (Genesis 3:21)? Surely the Lord would not hold the sons accountable for their father's sin! True, each person answers to God for his own sin; but every child born into the world is born a sinner because of Adam's sin. "Therefore, just as through one man [Adam] sin entered into the world, and death through sin, and so death spread to all men, because all sinned [in Adam]" (Romans 5:12).

Unfair? Of course not! Paul's argument in Romans 5 is

that this "one man" arrangement is an evidence of the
marvelous grace of God. If in one man, Adam, we are lost,
then in one man, Jesus Christ, we can be saved. By declaring all humanity guilty, God can bestow grace upon all
humanity in Jesus Christ. "For as in Adam all die, so also
in Christ all shall be made alive" (1 Corinthians 15:22).
Both Cain and Abel were lost sinners, and both needed
to be saved. But Cain refused to exercise faith; therefore,
God had to reject him. "And the Lord had regard for Abel
and for his offering; but for Cain and for his offering He
had no regard" (Genesis 4:4, 5).
Faith can be exercised only on the basis of some Word
from God. "So faith comes from hearing, and hearing by
the word of Christ" (Romans 10:17). Abel believed the
Word of God and acted upon it. What was that word?
That sinners needed to bring a blood sacrifice to the altar.
While it is true that the various sacrifices were not established ritually until the time of Moses, yet Genesis 3:21
implies that God Himself made the first animal sacrifices
in order to cover the first sinners. Long before the Law of
Moses, believers met God at the altar on the basis of a
blood sacrifice (Genesis 8:20-22; 15:1-11).
Cain did not come to the altar with a sacrifice of blood.
He was religious, but he was not righteous. Jude 11 calls
his religion "the way of Cain." Because God rejected
Cain, Cain rejected Abel and killed him. Then Cain lied
about the murder! No wonder 1 John 3:12 associates Cain
with "the evil one," because, like the devil, Cain was a
liar and a murderer (John 8:44). Satan's religion has
always been one of self-righteousness rather than faith
righteousness. This explains why both John the Baptist
and Jesus called the self-righteous Pharisees a "brood of
vipers" (Matthew 3:7; 12:34; 23:33).
Cain rejected salvation by faith, salvation through the
shed blood of a substitute. He wanted nothing to do with
blood, not unlike self-righteous religious people today.

Abel's faith was *saving* faith because he trusted God's
Word and the sacrifice that God ordained. He agreed with
Hebrews 9:22 that "without shedding of blood there is no
forgiveness."

The Church has been purchased by the blood of God's
Son (Acts 20:28). Believers are justified by His blood
(Romans 5:9). "In Him we have redemption through His
blood" (Ephesians 1:7). "To Him who loves us, and
released us from our sins by His blood" (Revelation 1:5).
The very praise in heaven centers on the sacrifice of Jesus
Christ: "Worthy is the Lamb that was slain" (Revelation
5:12).

"The way of Cain" is a popular way, because it appeals
to the ego of the sinner. "You don't need a substitute,"
Cain proudly announces. "You can make it by yourself!
To accept a sacrifice is to admit you're a sinner, and that
isn't really necessary. No need to humble yourself. Instead, accept yourself and be yourself! Your character and
good works will get you into heaven."

From the human point of view, Cain was a man of good
works and moral character. He labored in his field, he
came to the altar, and he brought God a sacrifice. But
from the divine viewpoint (and that is the one that
counts), Cain's "good works" were seen as "evil works."
"For this is the message which you have heard from the
beginning, that we should love one another; not as Cain,
who was of the evil one, and slew his brother. And for
what reason did he slay him? Because his deeds were
evil, and his brother's were righteous" (1 John 3:11, 12).
Religious worship and good works that do not spring
from faith in the heart are evil works in the eyes of God.
"For all of us have become like one who is unclean, and
all our righteous deeds are like a filthy garment" (Isaiah
64:6).

We enter the "race of faith," not by presenting our own
qualifications, but the qualifications of another—Jesus
Christ the Savior. We enter the race by admitting

that we are *not* qualified! This was Paul's experience
(Philippians 3:1-16) and it must also be ours.

2. HE HAD SACRIFICING FAITH.

Abel was not only a believer, but he was also a worshiper.
He was found at the altar, presenting his best, "the firstlings of his flock" (Genesis 4:4), to the Lord. Faith and
worship must go together, "for he who comes to God
must believe that He is, and that He is a rewarder of those
who seek Him" (Hebrews 11:6).

This chapter begins with a worshiper because worship
is the basis for everything else that we do in the life of
faith. Our witness, our work, even our daily walk, are all
by-products of worship. Wherever Abraham went in his
pilgrimage of faith, he pitched his tent *and built his altar*
(Genesis 12:8; 13:3, 4, 18). The tent was a testimony to the
world that he was a stranger on the earth, but the altar
witnessed that he was a citizen of heaven. The two must
go together.

But worship is not only an evidence of faith; it is also
an *essential* to faith. Our faith grows as we worship God.
Communion with God leads to confidence in God. One
of the problems in the church today is our lack of true
worship. Too often the sanctuary has become a theater
where paid performers entertain an audience. The audience pays the price by its patience during the sermon
and through offerings. Gone is the holy hush of God!
Gone is the awesome sense of His presence! In its place
is mere human enjoyment instead of spiritual enrich-
ment.

Abel brought the "firstlings of his flock," the very best
that he had. "Honor the Lord from your wealth, and from
the first of all your produce" (Proverbs 3:9). "But seek
first His kingdom and His righteousness" (Matthew
6:33). Too often we think first of ourselves, and we give to
God whatever may be left over, *if* we give to Him at all.

One Christian described this approach to life as "burning the candle to please ourselves and then blowing the smoke in God's face."

Today, we don't have tabernacles, temples, and altars. All true believers are God's priests (1 Peter 2:5), and it is our privilege to bring "spiritual sacrifices" to the Lord, the very best we have. The word "spiritual" doesn't mean "non-material," because what a Christian does with material wealth is very important to him and to God. "Spiritual" means "of a spiritual quality," set apart by the Spirit for God's glory. What are these sacrifices?

- *our bodies yielded to God* (Romans 12:1, 2)
- *sincere praise to God* (Hebrews 13:15)
- *good works for His glory* (Hebrews 13:16)
- *money and material things* (Philippians 4:10-18)
- *a broken heart* (Psalm 51:17)
- *prayer* (Psalm 141:2)

When the people of Israel returned to their land after the Babylonian exile, they at first experienced times of great economic distress. But then things began to look up and a measure of prosperity came to the land. It was then that they stopped giving their best to the Lord. God raised up the Prophet Malachi to accuse them. They were offering sick, lame, and blind animals as sacrifices (Malachi 1:8). "Why not offer it to your governor?" asked the prophet. "Would he be pleased with you?"

In modern terms, suppose I gave my wife a gift equivalent to the amount I give to the Lord; would she be happy? Would I really be showing love to her? We often make sacrifices in order to give nice things to loved ones, but we don't want to sacrifice in order to worship God with our best.

The word "worship" is a contraction of "worth-ship," that is, "ascribing worth to someone or something." When we worship God, we are ascribing worth to Him;

and the sacrifices we bring should be an indication of
that worth. Abel brought his best, and so should we.

3. HE HAD SUFFERING FAITH.

It costs to live by faith! Both the named and the unnamed
people in Hebrews 11 paid a price to trust God; but we
pay a *greater* price if we do *not* trust God!

There are three unbelievers named in this chapter:
Cain (11:4), Esau (11:20; and see 12:14-17), and Pharaoh
(11:23-29). These three men typify the three enemies of
the believer: *the world* (Pharaoh, for Egypt is a picture of
the world system), *the flesh* (Esau), and *the devil* (Cain,
"who was of the evil one" according to 1 John 3:12). The
world refuses to operate by faith because it claims that
"seeing is believing." The flesh opposes faith in God
because faith demands humility and dependence, and
the flesh wants to be proud and independent. Of course,
the devil attacks faith because faith gives us victory over
his deceptive devices.

Cain was willing to become a murderer in order to
protect himself from "losing face" and having to humble
himself before God. His values were twisted. Abel was
willing to sacrifice his life and suffer for his faith, because
Abel had the kind of values that really counted. He
would have agreed with martyred missionary Jim Elliot
who wrote, "He is no fool who gives what he cannot keep
to gain what he cannot lose."

While we certainly don't want to minimize the price
that the martyrs paid, it is sometimes more difficult to
live for the faith and suffer than to *die* for the faith. Think
of the suffering that Jeremiah endured at the hands of his
countrymen, or the suffering that Paul experienced as he
carried the gospel from city to city! In the Soviet sector of
the world today, there are hundreds of dedicated believers
who are suffering intensely because of their faith in Jesus
Christ. Suffering faith doesn't always lead to a firing

squad or an early grave. It could involve daily pressures and persecutions that make life almost unbearable.

How, then, is the suffering believer able to "take it" and keep going? *He has the approval of God.* God the Father bore witness to Abel's faith (Hebrews 11:4), and so did the Son (Matthew 23:35) and the Holy Spirit. Abel pleased God, and God rewarded Abel. Cain gained the world but lost his soul. Abel lost his life but gained the approval of God. Cain refused to shed the blood of a lamb so that he might please God, but he deliberately shed his brother's blood so that he might serve the devil!

If we live to please ourselves, we will always be the losers. If we live to please the world, we will not be able to please God. It's all a matter of values. Cain's values were those of the immediate, not the eternal. Abel lived for the eternal. Like Moses in a later century, Abel lived for the invisible, and he was not disappointed (Hebrews 11:26, 27).

The life of faith is not an easy life. God doesn't promise to shelter us or pamper us, but He does promise to encourage us and enable us as we go through the fire. To some of the heroes of faith, God gave marvelous deliverance; to others, He gave marvelous endurance. Peter was delivered from prison the night before his execution was to take place, but James was slain for his faith (Acts 12). It's not important that you and I know what God has planned for us. It is important that we trust Him and leave the future in His capable hands.

4. HE HAD SPEAKING FAITH.

What a remarkable testimony: ". . . through faith, though he is dead, he still speaks." Faith simply has to speak! "I believed, therefore I spoke" (2 Corinthians 4:13). When John the Baptist's father, Zacharias, refused to believe God, he was smitten with dumbness and unable to speak (Luke 1:18-23). In contrast, Mary believed God—and broke out into song (Luke 1:26-55)!

No words from Abel are recorded anywhere in the
Bible, yet this man, the first martyr, still speaks to us
today. His life speaks to us, as recorded in Genesis 4 and
Hebrews 11. God wrote down that Abel's deeds were
righteous (1 John 3:12). We speak with our lives as well as
with our lips. In fact, the two must go together if our
testimony is to be effective. We are certainly not saved by
good works (Ephesians 2:8-10), but good works ought to
be the evidence of our saving faith (James 2:14-26).

Abel's greatest witness was by his shed blood. Hebrews
12:18-24 contrasts Mt. Sinai on earth with Mt. Zion in
heaven, and among the contrasts given is that of the
blood of Jesus Christ and the blood of Abel (12:24). If the
blood of Jesus Christ bears witness to "better things,"
then the blood of Abel must at least bear witness of
"good things." This ties in with Genesis 4:10, where God
said to Cain, "The voice of your brother's blood is crying
to Me from the ground."

Abel's blood cried out from the earth, while the blood
of Jesus Christ bears witness from heaven. Abel's blood
cried out for judgment, while our Lord's blood speaks of
mercy and grace. Because of his brother's blood, Cain
was driven away from the face of God; but the blood of
Jesus Christ opens for us the way into the presence of
God (Hebrews 10:19-25). The blood of Abel makes us
think of death, while the blood of Jesus Christ speaks to
us of eternal life.

Many people today, even religious people, want to hear
nothing about blood. They want a "refined religion" that
has "purged itself" of the "pagan ideas" such as blood
sacrifices. But the Bible makes it clear that "without
shedding of blood there is no forgiveness" (Hebrews 9:22;
Leviticus 17:11). In a sense, Abel is speaking to us, not so
much about his own blood, but about the blood of the
Savior. He doesn't want us to linger over his blood, because that can only lead to despair. He wants us to trust
the blood of Jesus Christ and find eternal life and victory
over sin.

If we omit the blood, we silence God. If we oppose the blood, we rob God of the glory due to His name. In Hebrews 12:22-24, the blood is at the top of the list! Why? Because the ever-living Savior who died for us is exalted to the highest place in heaven. Abel is dead, but Christ is alive! Abel's blood cannot wash away our sins, but the blood of Jesus Christ can cleanse us from all iniquity (1 John 1:9). When our Lord arose from the dead, He retained in His body the wounds of Calvary, and these wounds have been glorified in heaven! That shows how much God values the blood of the Cross.

The way of Cain is the easy way, the popular way, the approved way of the world. But the way of Cain is the way of unbelief that leads to despair and judgment. Cain went out from God's presence and built a city (Genesis 4:16ff.), but Abel went to a heavenly city. Cain possessed many of the good things that life offered, but he didn't have God, because he didn't have faith. No matter what we may possess, if we don't have God, we don't have anything.

The way of Abel is the difficult way, the narrow way, the way of the Cross. It's the only saving way, the "new and living way" that Jesus opened for us when He died on Calvary. It leads to life.

Listen to the witness of Cain: "My punishment is too great to bear!" (Genesis 4:13).

Listen to the witness of Abel: "In Him [Jesus Christ] we have redemption through His blood, the forgiveness of our trespasses, according to the riches of His grace" (Ephesians 1:7).

Which witness will you receive?

3/ ENOCH: A FAITH FOR TOUGH TIMES
GENESIS 5:21–24; HEBREWS 11:5, 6; JUDE 14, 15

"I think I'll go to church with you today."

That remark from her husband startled this Christian wife, but she was happy for his decision. All wrapped up in business and making money, he appeared to have no interest in spiritual things.

On their way to church, the praying wife began to have second thoughts. What would the sermon be about? What would the Scripture readings be? Which Sunday was it on the church calendar? Maybe it would turn out to be the wrong Sunday! On arrival, she took one look at the order of service and felt her heart sink within her: the Scripture reading was Genesis 5! Her husband would have to sit through a long list of ancient names—and there was no gospel in Genesis 5!

But God had His purposes to work out, and her fears didn't hinder the Spirit. The husband sat through the service with apparent interest and a few weeks later was converted to Christ. When she asked him what it was in the service that started him thinking seriously about becoming a Christian, he replied, "That Scripture reading from Genesis. One phrase was repeated and I couldn't escape it: 'And he died.' I got to thinking about the reality of death, and I knew I needed a Savior."

But there is one man named in Genesis 5 who was an exception, about whom the Spirit could not write, "And he died." His name is Enoch—and he never died! One day God carried him off to heaven!

By the way, if we have started walking with God by trusting Christ as our Savior, then one day God may translate us to heaven "in a moment, in the twinkling of an eye" (1 Corinthians 15:52). I say *may* translate us, because we don't know when Jesus will return, and death may come first. Either way, we will be at home with the Lord.

Meanwhile, we must live in this wicked world: and that is just what Enoch's faith is all about. Enoch walked with God and kept his life pure during one of the most difficult times in world history—the period just before the Flood. It was a time of unparalleled ungodliness, when wickedness was increasing, corruption spreading, and violence breaking the heart of God (Genesis 6:1-13). Both Noah and Enoch were warning people of the wrath to come, but nobody was paying much attention (see Jude 14, 15, which also refers to our Lord's return to judge the world; and 2 Peter 2:5). People were enjoying life and making their plans as though nothing could interrupt them (Luke 17:27). Some Bible students think that Romans 1:18-32 is a description of the sinful degeneration of the human race just before the Flood.

Jesus said that the world before the Flood pictures the world before His return (Matthew 24:32ff.); so, in that sense, you and I are living in times not unlike those that Enoch lived in. Corruption and violence are on the increase, the number of the godly is on the decrease, and there appears to be no release! All of us need a faith for tough times if we ever hope to keep clean in a dirty world. The same spiritual resources that Enoch had are available to us today.

1. HE BELIEVED GOD (Hebrews 11:6).

The record in Genesis 5:21, 22 suggests that Enoch did not walk with God during the first sixty-five years of his life. We have no reason to believe that he was a wicked sinner, like most of the people around him. But he was still an unbeliever, and that is enough to condemn a man. God's warning to "moral sinners" today is: "He who believes in the Son has eternal life; but he who does not obey the Son shall not see life, but the wrath of God abides on him" (John 3:36). Judgment is over the sinner's head *right now!*

What was it that started Enoch trusting God and walking with God? It was the birth of his son, Methuselah. In my own pastoral ministry, I have seen similar things happen. The wonderful gift of life changes homes and hearts as mothers and fathers contemplate the privileges and responsibilities of parenthood.

But faith does not come from personal experiences; it comes from the divine Word of God (Romans 10:17). It is likely that God gave a special message to Enoch, a message that related somehow to the birth of his baby boy. This message awakened faith in Enoch's heart, and this faith transformed his life.

What was the message? It probably had something to do with the impending judgment that God would send over the earth. Most Hebrew lexicons and Bible encyclopedias tell us that the name "Methuselah" means "man of the dart" or "man of the javelin," suggesting that Enoch's son was a hunter. The fascinating thing about this man is that *he lived so long*—969 years, in fact! Perhaps his long life is a clue to the significance of his birth.

If we make the creation of Adam year 1, and calculate the years recorded in Genesis 5, we discover that Methuselah was born in the year 687 from the creation of Adam. If we add 969 to 687, we get a total of 1656, the number of the year in which Methuselah died.

If we continue our calculations, we discover that Noah was born in the year 1056 from the creation of Adam. Since Noah was 600 years old when the Flood came (Genesis 7:6), it means that the Flood came in the year 1656—the year that Methuselah died!

All of this is speculation, of course, but it could be that with the birth of his son, Enoch received a warning from God that judgment was coming. It was this revelation that turned him from careless unbelief to serious faith. He began to warn others about the wrath to come.

If we are going to keep clean in this dirty world, we must have faith in God's Word. Enoch believed God. He believed that there is a God and that this God rewards those who obey Him. If there is future judgment for sinners, there is also future reward for saints; and Enoch began to live for that reward. The Apostle Peter used this same motivation—future judgment and reward—as a basis for his admonition to the church that Christians live holy lives here and now (2 Peter 3:10-18). So did the Apostle John (1 John 2:28—3:3) and the Apostle Paul (Romans 13:11-14).

When we look around and see things getting worse—look up!

2. HE WALKED WITH GOD (Genesis 5:22).

The crisis of faith led to a process of faithfulness, and that's exactly as it should be. Spiritual birth ought to lead to spiritual growth. A step of faith should be but the beginning of a walk of faith. Noah walked with God (Genesis 6:9) and so did Abraham, Isaac, and Jacob (Genesis 48:15).

Often in the New Testament epistles, the Christian life is compared to a walk. We are commanded to "behave properly" (Romans 13:13), walk "by the Spirit" (Galatians 5:16), walk "in love" (Ephesians 5:2), and "walk in the light" (1 John 1:7). A walk begins with a step of faith, trusting Jesus Christ as Savior. A walk requires life.

Corpses don't walk! But walking also demands strength and the ability to stand. We can't walk unless we are free. In Jesus Christ, the believer has life, strength, and liberty. As we nourish our souls on the Word of God, and exercise ourselves in prayer, we develop the strength and direction needed for our daily walk with the Lord.

"Do two men walk together unless they have made an appointment?" asked the prophet Amos (3:3). The word translated "appointment" can also mean "agreement," and both meanings are important. If you and I are going to walk with God, we must begin the day with *an appointment*, a definite time set aside for reading the Bible, meditating on its truths, and praying for God's help to obey what we have learned. Unless we wait on God and worship God, we can never successfully walk with God.

"Can two walk together except they have made an agreement?" Enoch walked with God because he agreed with God. He agreed with what God said about the world around him. The key word in Enoch's sermons was *ungodly* (Jude 14, 15). In other words, Enoch was a separated man. He was *in* the world but he was not *of* the world. Enoch didn't mix himself with the worldly crowd and compromise his testimony. No doubt they ridiculed him, but Enoch maintained his godly walk in spite of godless opposition. (See 2 Corinthians 6:14—7:1.)

Malachi 2:6 gives a perfect description of what it means for the believer to walk with God: "True instruction was in his mouth, and unrighteousness was not found on his lips; he walked with Me in peace and uprightness, and he turned many back from iniquity." Enoch was carried to heaven before the Flood came, but he had the joy of knowing that his words and his walk had been a witness for God.

If we believe God, then we can walk with God. "Thy word is a lamp to my feet, and a light to my path" (Psalm 119:105). I thank God that early in my Christian experience, more experienced saints encouraged me to begin each day with the Lord. This is a "holy habit" that I have maintained by God's grace over these many years, and what a delight it has been! If we meet God in the morning, then we can walk with Him all the day long, no matter what the problems and pressures might be.

Walking with God is one of the best ways to stay out of sin and trouble. I read an interesting story about evangelist Dwight L. Moody that beautifully illustrates this truth. While he was living in Chicago, Moody received a special invitation to attend the grand opening of a "billiards emporium," which was nothing but a fancy name for a pool hall. Whatever merit may be attached to the game today, in Moody's day it was associated with the low practices of low people.

Moody went to the "emporium" the day before the opening, and he asked the manager, "When I come tomorrow, may I bring a Friend with me?" The man was hesitant; he knew Moody! "I never go anywhere without this Friend," said Moody, "and if I can't bring Him, I won't come at all." Moody then knelt down and prayed that the "emporium" would fail; and within a month, the place was out of business!

Abraham was walking with God, and was the "friend of God," so he stayed out of Sodom; but Lot was a friend of the world, so he moved into Sodom—with disastrous results (Genesis 18, 19). It pays to walk with God.

3. HE PLEASED GOD (Hebrews 11:5).
We face daily three possible motivations: we can please God, please ourselves, or please other people. If we live to please only ourselves, we will have a miserable life. (Read Romans 15:1-3.) If we live only to please people, we will have an even more miserable life, because we can never please everybody! All of us need to follow the example of Jesus Christ: "I always do the things that are pleasing to Him" (John 8:29).

It's unfortunate that so many Christians have the

mistaken idea that God is difficult to please. *He is not.*
He loves us and knows all about us. He wants the very
best for us. All of His resources are at our disposal. He is
patient with us. Because He knows the end from the
beginning, He can plan for us and work out His wonderful providences for our good and His glory. Our relationship with Him ought to be the most delightful thing in
all the world!

Hebrews 11:6 suggests that the first step toward pleasing God is to *seek Him.* This doesn't suggest that God is
hidden and must be found, or that He is far away and
must be located. To seek God means to desire Him with
all our hearts. It means to focus our affection and attention on God and to realize that nothing matters that is
outside God and His will for our lives. "As the deer pants
for the water brooks, so my soul pants for Thee, O God.
My soul thirsts for God, for the living God . . ." (Psalm
42:1, 2). That is the attitude of the believer who sincerely
seeks God.

God responds to the sincere, believing heart. "Then
you will call upon Me and come and pray to Me, and I
will listen to you. And you will seek Me and find Me,
when you search for Me with all your heart" (Jeremiah
29:12, 13). God seeks our fellowship and enjoys it, the
way a father or mother would enjoy time together with a
child, or a husband with his wife. There is a special delight in fellowship with God that the unsaved person and
the careless Christian know nothing about. If the first
step toward pleasing God is *seeking* Him, then the second
step is *enjoying* Him. "He has brought me to his banquet
hall, and his banner over me is love" (Song of Solomon 2:4).

The third step is *becoming like Him.* The Father is
pleased with His Son, Jesus Christ (Matthew 3:17); and
therefore He is pleased with us as we become like Him.
As we behold Jesus Christ in the Word, we become more
and more like Him (2 Corinthians 3:18). It is a fellowship
that transforms.

Keep in mind that Enoch was surrounded by a society that seemed prosperous and comfortable. During the three hundred years that he walked with God, Enoch was tempted to believe that the people around him were not such sinners after all. Judgment coming? What evidences were there that judgment was coming? The civilization that unbelieving Cain had founded was flourishing (Genesis 4:16-24). Only a madman would condemn such success and say that God was not pleased.

But Enoch walked by faith, not by sight. Like Christian in John Bunyan's *Pilgrim's Progress*, Enoch was not attracted by the cheap merchandise in the Vanity Fair of the world. He lived only to please God, and that motive kept him from being polluted by the world around him.

Living to please God is an evidence that we are walking by faith, investing our lives in the things that are eternal. Those who walk by sight want immediate recognition and immediate results. They battle their way through life, taking care of number one—self. They sacrifice the eternal for the temporary, character for empty praise, and success for passing fame. Enoch made none of those foolish blunders, because he lived to please God.

Was it easy? Of course not! Times were difficult, and it takes tough faith to keep going for God in tough times. But faith is like the muscles in our arms: the more we use our faith, the stronger it becomes. Just about the time we think we are defeated, God sends the victory; and then a brand new battle begins.

He is a rewarder of those who seek Him.

4. HE WENT TO BE WITH GOD.

"By faith Enoch was taken up . . . and he was not found because God took him up. . . ." Our familiar King James Version uses the word "translated," which simply means "to carry across." The Christian life begins with the miracle of "translation," according to Colossians 1:13:

"For He delivered us from the domain of darkness, and transferred us to the kingdom of His beloved Son." The Greek word was used to describe the deportation of prisoners of war to another land, such as when the Babylonians took the Jews to Babylon.

But our experience of salvation sets us free from bondage! We are transferred from Satan's dominion into the kingdom of Christ, a kingdom of love and light. Faith in Christ makes us the citizens of heaven and joint-heirs with the King of glory! We are not deported slaves; we are delivered sons of God.

The Christian life is a life of deliverance and freedom. The unbelieving people in the world consider themselves to be free, but they are really in bondage. They look at Christians and feel sorry for us because they think we are in bondage, when actually we are free! No doubt Enoch's neighbors pitied him because he didn't get involved in the pleasures that fascinated them. They didn't realize that Enoch was enjoying life in a kingdom of love and light, while they were enslaved in a kingdom of death, darkness, and utter destruction.

Enoch had solved the ultimate problem—death. Until a person has learned to die, he hasn't really learned to live. But Enoch did not die! He was certainly prepared to die, but God had other plans for him. "I am ready to meet my Maker," said Sir Winston Churchill on his seventy-fifth birthday. "Whether my Maker is prepared for the great ordeal of meeting me is another matter." Enoch was ready to meet God and God was ready to meet Enoch.

In fact, Enoch had been walking with God for so many years that his transfer to heaven was not even an interruption. Enoch had been practicing Colossians 3 centuries before Paul wrote the words: ". . . keep seeking the things above. . . . Set your mind on the things above, not on the things that are on earth" (vv. 1, 2). One moment Enoch was on earth, and the next moment he was gone. There is a hint in Hebrews 11:5 that some people went looking for him but were unable to find him. A similar thing happened when God took the prophet Elijah to heaven (2 Kings 2).

Without pressing the image too far, we can see in Enoch's translation a picture of what will happen to the Church when Jesus Christ returns (1 Thessalonians 4:13-18). One day, millions of people, believers in Jesus Christ, will suddenly vanish, "in a moment, in the twinkling of an eye" (1 Corinthians 15:52). If you and I have been walking with God and seeking to please Him, then our transfer to heaven will not surprise us or introduce us to a spiritual element that is foreign to us. I trust that, like Enoch, we will require very few "adjustments" to feel at home in heaven.

It is important to note that Enoch didn't go to heaven because he walked with God. He went to heaven because he believed God, and it was this faith that made his walk what it was. The New Testament makes a distinction between going to heaven (salvation) and rewards in heaven (sanctification and service). God is "a rewarder of those who seek Him" (Hebrews 11:6). To seek Him means to seek to please Him, to serve Him; and God rewards those who faithfully obey Him and serve Him. "For we shall all stand before the judgment seat of God. . . . So then each one of us shall give account of himself to God" (Romans 14:10, 12).

It isn't likely that Enoch knew that God was going to take him to heaven in such a dramatic way. At least we have no evidence from Scripture that God had revealed this to him. However, you and I as believers in Jesus Christ do know that one day we may be raptured to glory. And the daily expectation of seeing Jesus and going to heaven ought to make a difference in the way we live. The "blessed hope" of the return of the Savior ought to motivate us to faithfulness in service (Luke 12:35-48) as well as purity in conduct (1 John 2:28—3:3).

For the unbeliever, the future holds nothing but judgment. That was the theme of Enoch's message to the careless people in his day. "Behold, the Lord came with many thousands of His holy ones, to execute judgment upon all, and to convict all the ungodly of all their ungodly deeds which they have done in an ungodly way, and of all the harsh things which ungodly sinners have spoken against Him" (Jude 14, 15).

Enoch's experience is evidence of the reality of heaven. Where did he go? He went to heaven! James M. Barrie, the creator of *Peter Pan*, once wrote, "Heaven for climate, hell for company." But there will be no "company" in hell, because hell is a place of eternal loneliness. The selfishness of the people in hell will prevent them from wanting to contribute anything to the comforts of others. Only in heaven will there be love and fellowship. The person who sneers, "Well, I don't mind going to hell! I'll have lots of company!" doesn't understand the awfulness of sin or the loneliness of hell.

Enoch encourages us to keep going in tough times. If God is walking with us, we need not fear the world around us. If heaven lies before us, we need not despair at the crumbling society and the hopelessness that lie before us. If we, like Enoch, will believe God, walk with God, and seek to please God, then one day we shall rejoice and be rewarded when we go to be with God.

A faith for tough times: "and this is the victory that has overcome the world—our faith" (1 John 5:4).

4/ NOAH: TOTAL FAITH
GENESIS 6—9;
HEBREWS 11:7

The word *holistic* appeared originally in 1926, but in more recent years it has taken on new importance. General Jan Christiaan Smuts published a book called *Holism and Evolution,* and today we seem to have "holistic" approaches to almost everything from medicine to jogging. Book titles such as *Total Fitness* remind us that the concept is still helping to generate new applications of an old idea.

Perhaps "holistic medicine" can give us our best illustration of this concept. Many doctors believe that the healing of the patient involves much more than the application of medicines or surgery to the human body. Healing also involves the attitudes of the patient, his nutrition, and his environment. Studies suggest that depression and grief can trigger sickness and even promote the growth of certain kinds of cancer, while a happy and positive attitude can encourage healing.

This concept of "holism" also applies to the Christian life, and it is illustrated in the experience of Noah, the man who built the ark and rescued himself and seven others from the Flood. You can see this holism at work when you examine the characteristics of Noah's faith.

1. HIS FAITH INVOLVED THE WHOLE PERSON.
To begin with, Noah's *mind* was involved, because God
warned him that the Flood was coming. The Greek word
used here carries with it the idea of instruction as well as
warning. God not only told Noah what was going to
happen, but He also told him how to deal with it. Noah
was "divinely instructed" by God, and this was what
saved him and his family. One cannot separate faith from
the Word of God (Romans 10:17).

Genesis 6:9 makes it clear that Noah was already a
believer when God warned him about the coming judgment. Because of his faith, Noah was "a righteous man";
and because of his faithfulness in his walk with God,
Noah was "blameless in his time." Noah and his family
were among that dwindling number of true believers in a
violent and corrupt age, an elect fellowship that num-
bered only eight when the Flood came (1 Peter 3:20).
According to the figures given in Genesis 5, Noah was
born in the year 1056 since the creation of Adam, and
died in the year 2006 (Genesis 9:28, 29).

Why did God reveal His plan to Noah and instruct him
how to escape judgment? "But Noah found favor in the
eyes of the Lord" (Genesis 6:8). Salvation is always by
grace! No man deserves to be saved. It is only by the
mercy of God that we are not consumed.

True faith must involve the mind; we must hear a word
from God if we are to have something to believe. But true
faith also involves *the emotions*. Noah was "moved with
fear" (Hebrews 11:7, KJV). The NASB translates this
single Greek participle as "in reverence." In classical
Greek the word meant "caution, vigilence, concern,"
words that certainly have emotional overtones. "Reveren-
tial piety" is a good translation; "the fear of the Lord."

Faith that is purely emotional is based on feeling, not
fact. But faith that is not emotional, that ignores the
feelings of the heart, is purely intellectual and not motiva-
tional. Even the demons "shudder" when they believe

(James 2:19). A cold intellectual kind of faith never achieved the great victories listed in Hebrews 11!

Fear is a legitimate emotion, and it probably motivates people far more than they realize. We use fear to warn our children about the dangers of accidents on the streets, electricity, fire, and even poison. While the fear of being found out may not be the highest motive for doing right, at least it keeps some people from doing wrong. Fear of death sends us to the doctor for an annual checkup and to the checkbook for an annual premium to be sent to the insurance company.

Faith must grip the heart as well as enlighten the mind. The judgment God promised to send was an entirely new thing: rain from heaven. Genesis 2:5, 6 indicates that God watered the earth by means of springs, rivers, and a system of evaporation and condensation. Some scientists believe that there was a "water canopy" over the earth, and this helped to keep a uniform temperature on the land mass (Genesis 1:6-8). With the coming of the Flood, this "canopy" was dispersed as rain when "the floodgates of the sky were opened" (Genesis 7:11). No matter how God accomplished the event, rain was a new thing to the people of the earth.

Did the neighbors laugh at Noah? Did they think that the construction of a huge bargelike ship was a foolish thing? It had to take something more than mere intellectual faith to motivate Noah and his family to obey God. Their hearts were stirred by a godly fear, for judgment was going to come.

Faith that informs the mind and stirs the heart must also motivate *the will*. Noah proved his faith in that he "prepared an ark." God gave Noah all the necessary instructions and Noah obeyed them to the letter. I have already pointed out that true Bible faith means obeying God in spite of circumstances (dry land and no rain) and consequences (ridicule and unbelief as the years passed). Genesis 6:3 informs us that God patiently waited 120

years before He sent the Flood (see 1 Peter 3:20); and
2 Peter 2:5 reminds us that, during this time, Noah was
preaching the Word of righteousness to an unbelieving
population. Nobody can blame God for the multitudes
that perished: they had plenty of opportunity to trust the
Lord.

Yes, Noah's faith involved the whole person. It was not
the intellectual faith of the professor or the emotional
faith of the fanatic. It was the balanced faith of a true
believer. Noah received God's revelation in his mind, he
was stirred in his heart by godly fear, and he obeyed what
God told him to do. Obedience without faith is presump-
tion. Faith without obedience is pretense. Noah obeyed
God because his inner person was committed to the Lord.

2. HIS FAITH INFLUENCED THE WHOLE FAMILY.
Noah's obedient faith brought about "the salvation of his
household." This doesn't mean that Noah's wife, sons,
and daughters-in-law were saved by proxy, because each
lost sinner must trust the Lord for himself and exercise
personal saving faith. From the very beginning of the
ministry of the Church, the gospel message was ad-
dressed to the entire family, all who were able to hear
and believe. "For the promise is for you and your children," Peter announced at Pentecost (Acts 2:39). This was
his message to the relatives and friends of Cornelius
(Acts 11:13, 14), and it was Paul's message in Corinth
(Acts 18:8) and Philippi (Acts 16:14, 15, 31). The faith of
the head of the household led the way for the household
to believe and be saved.

Three questions in the book of Genesis summarize the
matter: "Where are you?" (3:9); "Where is . . . your
brother?" (4:9); and "Where is . . . your wife?" (18:9).
Once I trust Jesus Christ as my Savior, I have an obligation
to share the Word with my brother, my wife, and the other

members of my family. Noah's faith was not "transferable," but it was contagious!

There is a frightening contrast between Noah and Lot (Genesis 19) when it comes to their influence on their family. Because Noah trusted God and walked with God, he was able to win his own loved ones to the Lord. Lot was a believer, but he didn't walk with God. When he tried to warn his family of the coming judgment, they only laughed at him (Genesis 19:14). Lot's wife disobeyed God and was judged instantly. Lot's daughters involved their drunken father in incest and gave birth to the two great enemies of the nation of Israel, the Ammonites and the Moabites. Lot's compromise destroyed his family; Noah's conviction and consecration saved his family.

The first place a man or woman ought to have spiritual influence is in his or her own family. Andrew trusted Christ and went and found his brother Simon and brought him to Jesus (John 1:35-42). This doesn't mean that we must first win our family before we can attempt to win anybody else, but it does mean that the believer ought to start at home and maintain a good witness there. What Jesus said to the newly converted man of Gadara should be taken to heart by every believer: "Go home to your people and report to them what great things the Lord has done for you, and how He had mercy on you" (Mark 5:19).

The three sons of Noah would be the founders of the nations of the earth. They and their wives would be fruitful and fill the earth with their descendants. At least at the beginning, the families of the earth would all be believers. Sad to say, their descendants would ultimately turn from God; and God's response would be the calling of Abraham and the establishing of a godly line.

If our faith involves our total person—mind, heart, and will—then it will be difficult to keep it from influencing the people around us, especially those who live with us.

Believing fathers and mothers have the priceless privilege of influencing their children, and their children's children, in the things of the Lord. Moses said it best:

"And these words, which I am commanding you today, shall be on your heart; and you shall teach them diligently to your sons and shall talk of them when you sit in your house and when you walk by the way and when you lie down and when you rise up" (Deuteronomy 6:6, 7).

3. HIS FAITH INDICTED THE WHOLE WORLD.

The record says "by which [faith] he condemned the world." We have already discovered what kind of world Noah lived in, one filled with wickedness, corruption, and violence. By his walk, his work, and his witness, Noah condemned the society around him. The prophet Ezekiel used Noah as an example of righteous witness in a decadent age (14:14); and Peter used Noah's preaching as proof that God witnesses before He judges (2 Peter 2:5). "For the coming of the Son of Man will be just like the days of Noah," said Jesus in the great Olivet Discourse (Matthew 24:37ff.); and He pointed out some of the characteristics of Noah's neighbors.

They were careless (Matthew 24:38). Judgment was coming, and yet they were involved in the everyday activities of life. There is certainly nothing wrong with eating or getting married, but in this case the good crowded out the best. Noah and his three sons were married men, but this didn't hinder them from trusting God and preparing for the impending Flood. Noah's concern and conviction condemned the complacency and carelessness of the world.

They were ignorant (Matthew 24:39). "They did not understand" until it was too late, and they were all taken away in death. It is a key doctrine of the Christian life that "By faith we understand . . ." (Hebrews 11:3). Noah's unsaved neighbors could have understood God's truth if only they had wanted to. Noah's understanding of God's plan condemned their ignorance.

They were unbelieving. Noah's faith condemned their unbelief. Noah preached the truth to them, but they refused to hear it. Can't you hear them laughing as they asked, "What is rain? What is a flood? Why are you building a big vessel on dry land?" The unsaved world says, "Seeing is believing!" and goes on in its futile thinking, only to discover too late that God was right after all.

They were proud and self-confident. Peter used the story of Noah (among other things) to emphasize the fact that God does fulfill His promises, no matter how long He may wait (2 Peter 3:1ff.). Twelve decades went by before the Flood came, and the scoffers increased in number and in brazen self-confidence with each passing year. "Everything is going on just as it was!" they taunted Noah and his family. "Where is your promised judgment?" *But it came,* just as the day of the Lord will come when men are saying to each other, "Peace and safety!" (1 Thessalonians 5:1ff.).

During that period of building and preaching, Noah won no converts, only his own family. How discouraged he could have been! But God doesn't measure ministry by numerical success; He measures it by faithfulness. By the time the period of grace was ended, not a person on earth could argue that God had not given him opportunity to be saved from judgment. Every mouth was stopped.

It is possible that many unbelieving people assisted Noah and his family in the construction of the ark. They could have been helping them gather materials, or possibly assisting in the actual building of the vessel. Imagine their condemnation! They would hear the Word day after day, and yet would reject it! I'm tempted to apply this to the lives of people today who go to church, even give to religious projects—those who know the truth of the

Word, and yet have rejected the Savior. Think of the condemnation they will experience at the judgment!

Noah was a witness, not a judge. God was the Judge, and God had already passed sentence on a wicked world. He was only waiting in the execution of the sentence. How patient the Lord is, "not wishing for any to perish but for all to come to repentance" (2 Peter 3:9). Believers today are to be witnesses, declaring by word and by action that faith in Jesus Christ is something real and life-changing. Our *visible* faith, our *victorious* faith, ought to condemn the whole world.

4. HIS FAITH INHERITED THE WHOLE BLESSING.
God rewards those who trust Him and diligently obey Him, and God rewarded Noah. He "became an heir of the righteousness which is according to faith" (Hebrews 11:7). Noah's righteousness came by faith (Genesis 6:9; 7:1) just as our righteousness must come by faith (Roman 4). Noah could not have been saved by keeping the law, because the law had not yet been given. Like Abraham, he "believed in the Lord; and He reckoned it to him as righteousness" (Genesis 15:6).

But righteousness involves much more than salvation from judgment; it makes the believer spiritually rich. Jesus Christ is the "heir of all things" (Hebrews 1:2); and when we trust Him, we become sharers in His inheritance. By faith we are children of God, "and if children, heirs also, heirs of God and fellow heirs with Christ" (Romans 8:17).

The salvation of Noah and his family was not simply temporal and physical—deliverance from the Flood; it was eternal and spiritual—release from sin and eternal wrath. God has promised that there will be no more global judgments by water (Genesis 9:8-17); the next global judgment will be by fire (2 Peter 3:7-13). However, the lost sinner needs to be saved from *eternal* judgment, the lake of fire (Revelation 20:11-15); and the only way to be saved is through faith in Jesus Christ.

How rich we are because of Jesus Christ! He was made poor that we might be made rich (2 Corinthians 8:9). We possess "every spiritual blessing in the heavenly places in Christ" (Ephesians 1:3), and this includes the riches of His grace (Ephesians 1:7), the riches of His glory (Ephesians 1:18), unfathomable riches (Ephesians 3:8), and "the depth of the riches both of the wisdom and knowledge of God" (Romans 11:33). Measured by the values of this world, Christians appear to be poor; but measured by the eternal values of heaven, we are the richest of all people!

When Noah stepped out of the ark, he was the monarch of a new earth. One day, God's people shall inherit "new heavens and a new earth, in which righteousness dwells" (2 Peter 3:13). We shall enter into the fullness of the inheritance and shall enjoy it for eternity!

The faith of Noah was total faith.

Is your faith *total* faith?

5/ ABRAHAM: NO FORWARDING ADDRESS
HEBREWS 11:8–10, 13–16

In October 1824, William Thompson entered the Glasgow University. The remarkable thing is that William Thompson was only ten years old! We know him today as Lord Kelvin, the man whose research into electricity helped to open up a new world for mankind.

About the year 1950 B.C., an old man of seventy-five enrolled in "The School of Faith." His name was Abram, later to be changed to Abraham. He stayed in "The School of Faith" for one hundred years, and ever since, people who want to walk by faith have been learning from him and his wife. Abraham and Sarah opened up a whole new world for all of us who have trusted Jesus Christ and are students in "The School of Faith."

Nearly one-third of the verses in Hebrews 11 are devoted to Abraham and Sarah. In fact, Abraham is named seventy-four times in the New Testament. Even today, he is revered by Jews, Muslims, and Christians. He has a great name today, but it is likely that his name was laughed at when he left Ur of the Chaldees and started to walk by faith—because when he left, *he didn't know where he was going!*

My wife is the navigator in our family, because I get lost in a parking lot. Whenever we leave home for a trip, I can be sure that she has checked the maps, researched the roads, and investigated the available accommodations. We always know where we are going, how we will get there, and how long it will take. But not so with Abraham and Sarah! When they said good-bye to their friends and relatives, they left no forwarding address. They were learning to live by faith. Instead of being citizens of Ur of the Chaldees (a very great city), they became "strangers and exiles on the earth" (11:13). They were not fugitives, running away from home, or vagabonds, looking for a home. They were "strangers" because they were away from home; and they were "pilgrims" because they were headed for home!

God accomplished some wonderful things in and through Abraham and Sarah, simply because they walked by faith and lived as pilgrims and strangers. God will do wonderful things in and through us today, if only we will become pilgrims and strangers. What are the characteristics of the Christian who is really living as a pilgrim and a stranger?

1. LISTENING EARS (Hebrews 11:8a).

"So faith comes from hearing, and hearing by the word of Christ" (Romans 10:17). God appeared to Abraham (Acts 7:2) and spoke to Abraham (Genesis 12:1ff.). This was purely an act of grace because Abraham and his family were all idolaters (Joshua 24:2). Abraham heard God's Word and that Word generated faith in his heart.

One of my professors at seminary said, "If a person listens to the Word long enough, he will do one of two things: either trust Christ and be saved, or reject it completely. Give people time to hear." I recall leading a man to Christ who, Sunday after Sunday for twenty years or

more, had listened to the former pastor minister the
Word. Indeed, it did take time!
We get the impression that Abraham trusted the Word
immediately. God spoke to him and God called him.
From that time, Abraham and Sarah kept their ears tuned
to hear the voice of God. As you read the story of their
lives in Genesis 12—25, you note the repeated phrase,
"And the word of the Lord came to Abraham. . . ."
Whenever Abraham acted apart from that Word, he got
himself into trouble (Genesis 12:10ff.; 16:1ff.). Whenever
he heard God's Word and obeyed it, he was successful
and God blessed him.

Believers today need to cultivate "ears of faith." Sometimes God speaks to us as we meditate on the Word.
Sometimes He speaks to us through the voice of a friend,
a pastor, or a Sunday school teacher. Often the Lord has
spoken to my wife and me as we have listened to a sermon. After church, we will compare notes and discover
that He has given both of us the same directions!

A true pilgrim goes through life attentive to the voice of
the Lord. Of course, we today don't hear the *audible*
voice of God; but the spiritual impression is just as real.
Even when asleep, a mother can hear the slightest sound
from her baby; and a true pilgrim can hear God speak in
the midst of the demands of life. "He who has ears, let
him hear" (Matthew 13:9).

2. OBEDIENT FEET (Hebrews 11:8b, 9).
Faith does more than listen; it acts, and it acts immediately. "By faith Abraham . . . obeyed. . . ." The Word
of God not only generates faith, it also gives the believer
the power to do what God has commanded. Mere intellectual faith, or emotional faith, will never lead to obedience.
But when the whole person is yielded to God, then
power is available for obedience. "For nothing will be

impossible with God" (Luke 1:37). I especially like the translation of this verse in the American Standard Version of 1901: "For no word from God shall be void of power." God's commandments are still God's enablements.

When Abraham and Sarah obeyed, they did not know where they were going! The *life* of faith begins with a *step* of faith. Abraham and Sarah obeyed God a step at a time, a day at a time, and God led them to their appointed destination. Even with detailed directions and a map, I often have difficulty arriving at my destination. Imagine what it would be like to travel along and not know where your destination lay!

God's pilgrims must have obedient feet because they are on the move. They must also live in tents. If they lived in permanent dwellings, it would be impossible for them to move at the command of God. This explains why you often find Abraham's *tent* mentioned in the Genesis story. According to Genesis 12:8, when he arrived in Canaan, Abraham pitched his tent between Bethel and Ai. Lot pitched his tent toward Sodom, and eventually moved into Sodom and abandoned his tent (Genesis 13:12; 14:12); but Abraham pitched his tent near Mamre ("fatness") and Hebron ("fellowship") and fellowshiped with God (Genesis 13:18).

It is a dangerous thing when a Christian starts to feel he is permanently "fixed" in this world. As pilgrims and exiles, we must feel "detached," ready to move at any moment. After all, we do live in temporary dwellings! "For we know that if the earthly tent which is our house is torn down, we have a building from God [our glorified body], a house not made with hands, eternal in the heavens" (2 Corinthians 5:1). At any time, without warning, your "tent" could be taken down in death—or taken up in glory, should the Savior return.

Since our citizenship is in heaven (Philippians 3:20, 21), we must not get too attached to this present world and what it has to offer. We must beware of *friendship* with this world (James 4:4), because it might lead to *love* of the world (1 John 2:15-17). If we start to love the world, we will become *conformed* to the world (Romans 12:2), and we might end up seeing everything we live for *condemned* with the world (1 Corinthians 11:32). This is what happened to Lot and his family. Lot forsook his tent and moved into Sodom, and everything he lived for went up in smoke (see 1 Corinthians 3:10-15).

This doesn't mean, of course, that Christians should become careless about their responsibilities in this world. The fact that we have the assurance of heaven ought to motivate us to be better neighbors, citizens, and workers. Abraham got involved in labor problems (Genesis 13), battles (Genesis 14), and even local water projects (Genesis 21:22ff.). He was separated, not isolated. He even entered into an alliance with some of the chiefs of the land (Genesis 14:13).

Whenever Abraham forsook his tent, he got into trouble. He left his tent at Bethel and went down to Egypt, and there God had to chasten him (Genesis 12:10-20). It was not until he returned to his tent that Abraham restored his fellowship with God. Somehow our motives and values get confused when we start to live "permanently" and forget that we are only temporary pilgrims and strangers in this world.

The word *promise* is repeated twice in Hebrews 11:9 and again in verse 13. It is an important word in the vocabulary of faith. God's pilgrims do not live on explanations; they live on promises. When God called Abraham, He did not give him a long explanation of what He had planned for him. Instead, He simply gave him a promise (Genesis 12:1-3) and He expected Abraham to live on the basis of that promise until a further revelation was given. At the time, it seemed like the fulfillment of the promise was impossible; but that's where faith came in. Abraham obeyed God when he did not know *where* or *how*.

The beautiful thing about faith is that it grows as we

obey. The "muscles of faith" are exercised by obedience, not by speculation or discussion. Like any other faculty, faith is strengthened by use. Abraham "grew strong in faith" (Romans 4:20), even though he made mistakes and occasionally acted in unbelief. The great heroes of faith were not perfect people, but they are *maturing* people. In spite of their weaknesses and blunders, they kept trusting and obeying, and God honored them.

The Christian life must grow "from faith to faith" (Romans 1:17). Saving faith is just the beginning. "But the righteous will live by his faith" (Habakkuk 2:4). It isn't enough to trust God to save us. We must also trust Him to keep us, to provide for our needs, to guide us in decisions, and to accomplish in and through us all that He has planned. When we recall that Abraham and Sarah did not have the written Word of God as we do today, then we can see how truly remarkable their faith was.

What was it that helped to keep them going?

3. STEADY EYES (Hebrews 11:10, 13a, 14).
You can always tell one of God's pilgrims by his or her eyes. They are not fixed on the artificial glory of the world around them, but on the heavenly glory of the world before them. Their attention, affection, and ambition are fixed on the things of God in the heavenly realm, not the things of man here on earth (see Colossians 3:1ff.). As we have seen from Abraham's example, this kind of posture didn't make them so "heavenly minded they were no earthly good." Abraham and Sarah were not distracted from life by their heavenly vision; they were directed in life.

For what and *at* what were they looking? They were looking for a city (Hebrews 11:10) and a country (11:14). They had forsaken their wealthy earthly city and were looking for a heavenly city. They had journeyed to a strange country because they were headed for a glorious

country. The only real estate Abraham owned in Canaan
was a burial cave; and yet he knew that the whole land
belonged to him and his descendants, because that was
what God had promised. He knew that his true citizenship was heavenly, not earthly; and he kept his attention
on that heavenly goal.

Sin came into this world when our first parents shifted
their attention from the heavenly to the earthly. "When
the woman saw that the tree was good for food . . ."
(Genesis 3:6). When Abraham saw that there was a famine
in the land, he took his eyes off the heavenly goal and
hurried into Egypt for protection. It was when Lot "lifted
up his eyes" and saw the plush valley of Jordan and the
exciting city of Sodom that he stopped living like a
pilgrim and started living for earthly things (Genesis
13:10ff.). There is no escaping the fact that *outlook* helps
to determine *outcome*. If you want to live a godly life, you
have to focus your attention on the things of God.

It is the vision of faith that makes possible the victory
of faith. Where we are looking determines *how* we are
living. "And this is the victory that has overcome the
world—our faith" (1 John 5:4). Faith enables us to see the
invisible (Hebrews 11:1), but when we start to focus on
the visible, we start to falter and fail. "While we look not
at the things which are seen, but at the things which are
not seen; for the things which are seen are temporal, but
the things which are not seen are eternal" (2 Corinthians
4:18).

The great achievers in history have been the men and
women who could see the invisible and strive to reach it.
Explorers, inventors, liberators, and pioneers in every
field have always been characterized by the steady eye
that sees the invisible and strives for the seemingly
impossible. "Faith is to believe what you do not yet see,"
wrote St. Augustine; "the reward for this faith is to see
what you believe."

The steady eye of faith keeps us going when the going

is tough. As the Latin proverb puts it, "When the pilot does not know what port he is heading for, no wind is the right wind." Abraham and Sarah experienced many trials and testings in "The School of Faith," but they pressed on and reached their goal. Leonardo da Vinci wrote in his notebook, "Every obstacle yields to stern resolve. He who is fixed to a star does not change his mind."

All of the achievers listed in Hebrews 11 had their eyes of faith fixed on the goal, because that's the only way you can run the race of faith. "I press on toward the goal for the prize of the upward call of God in Christ Jesus" (Philippians 3:14). They saw the opportunities, not the obstacles or the opposition. Most important of all, *they saw God.* That was what kept Moses going, "for he endured, as seeing him who is invisible" (Hebrews 11:27, KJV).

It is this glorious vision that keeps the race of faith from becoming dull and monotonous. Our greatest danger is *distraction.* How easy it is for us to take our eyes off the heavenly vision and fix them on some lesser thing. Then that "lesser thing" becomes a much bigger thing and starts to hinder us from running the race. Obstacles, after all, are those bothersome things we see *when we get our eyes off the goal.* Peter took his eyes off the Lord because he was distracted by the wind and the waves, and he began to sink (Matthew 14:30ff.).

Distractions lead to *detours,* and detours can gradually take us off course. The subtle thing about detours is that, while we are on them, we really think we are heading for our destination. We assure ourselves that the main road is just ahead. Detours have a way of slowing us down. In fact, the scenery around the detour may be more attractive than the scenery we see from the main road. But we aren't running the race to look at scenery! God has a goal for us to reach, and the detours only keep us from the goal or hinder us from reaching it sooner.

The pages of history are filled with the stories of gifted men and women who achieved nothing because they never organized their lives around a controlling purpose, a magnificent vision. Some people see nothing as they go through life; others see only what society wants them to see. Both of these might just as well be blind! But there have always been those chosen few who have caught the vision from God and run the race to reach the goal. They are not "disobedient to the heavenly vision" (Acts 26:19). Unbelief sees problems; faith sees potential. Unbelief sees obstacles; faith sees opportunities. The glory of the heavenly vision adds luster to even the dullest tasks. Men and women of faith are not always soaring; sometimes they are plodding. It is then that they need to see the heavenly vision even clearer, so that they might "walk, and not faint" (Isaiah 40:31, KJV).

Open ears, obedient feet, steady eyes: these are three marks of the true pilgrim.

4. READY LIPS (Hebrews 11:13b, 14).

God's pilgrims are not only walking; they are also talking. You can always identify a pilgrim by his readiness to share with others the vision that controls his life.

To begin with, the pilgrim is not ashamed to admit that he is a pilgrim. Like Christian in Bunyan's *Pilgrim's Progress*, the modern-day pilgrim tells those he meets that he is on his way to the heavenly city. He is not ashamed of his tent because he is heading for "the city which has foundations, whose architect and builder is God" (11:10). As George Morrison said, "The important thing is not what we live in but what we look for."

The lost can't hear what we are hearing or see what we are seeing. However, they can watch what we are doing (obedient feet) and hear what we are saying (ready lips). The two go together. There is no sense in witnessing about my heavenly calling if my earthly conduct is no different from that of the people to whom I am witnessing. The world is seeking reality, not hypocrisy.

But it is also true that a godly life *without verbal witness* may be just as ineffective in reaching others for Christ. They can see that we are different; but unless we tell them, they will never know *why* we are different. God's pilgrims must have that inner compulsion to share the Word of life. "For we cannot stop speaking what we have seen and heard" (Acts 4:20). We must be "ready always to give an answer to every man that asketh you a reason of the hope that is in you" (1 Peter 3:15, KJV).

Furthermore, God's pilgrims are not ashamed to admit that they are seeking the heavenly country, their own country (Hebrews 11:14). They are not embarrassed to sing:

This world is not my home,
I'm just a-passing through!

Lot was content to settle down in Sodom, but Abraham had to keep moving, following the heavenly vision. Lot was willing to sacrifice his daughters to the lust of the worldly crowd; while Abraham put his only son on the altar and dedicated him to God. Lot lost his personal witness, even with his own family; while Abraham's witness blessed his home, his nation, and today blesses all who, by faith, are the "children of Abraham."

Unbelievers simply don't know what we pilgrims are talking about. "They are from the world; therefore they speak as from the world, and the world listens to them. We are from God; he who knows God listens to us; he who is not from God does not listen to us. By this we know the spirit of truth and the spirit of error" (1 John 4:5, 6).

The mystic is so engrossed by the vision that he loses himself in it and forgets that there are helpless prisoners around him. But the true pilgrim is so encouraged by the

vision that he expresses himself in praise and witness
and seeks to take others with him. Like Moses, we say to
others, "Come with us and we will do you good, for the
Lord has promised good concerning Israel" (Numbers
10:29).

When our witness has to be manufactured, when it
doesn't flow from us in a simple, loving way, then we
have probably lost the glory of the vision, or perhaps we
have stumbled somewhere in our walk. Closed (or di-
verted) eyes and disobedient feet have a way of silencing
the tongue of the man or woman of faith. Zacharias didn't
believe God, and his voice was silenced (Luke 1:18-23).
Mary believed God, and her voice broke forth in song
(Luke 1:46-55). "We also believe, therefore also we speak"
(2 Corinthians 4:13).

An unashamed, unaffected witness is the result of an
unclouded vision and an uncluttered walk; and they, in
turn, depend on an undivided heart.

5. A DEDICATED HEART (Hebrews 11:15, 16).
The ears hear and the eyes see whatever the heart loves.
"Watch over your heart with all diligence, for from it flow
the springs of life" (Proverbs 4:23). If, as with Lot, the
heart secretly loves the world, then the eyes will see
Sodom, not heaven. The mouth eventually speaks the
things that are treasured in the heart. Jesus made that
clear: "For the mouth speaks out of that which fills the
heart" (Matthew 12:34).

The human heart contains a compass, and North is
whatever the heart loves the most. The believers in Hebrews 11 desired the better country, the heavenly country,
and this desire motivated and directed their lives. They
were always moving forward. They buried the alternatives.

Because their hearts were centered on the heavenly,
they had no desire to return to the life they had left

behind. This is a significant truth and emphasizes the message of Hebrews, which is "let us press on to maturity" (6:1). The life of faith is a life of growth; it produces giants. The life of unbelief is a stunted life; it produces midgets. Abraham would have been a successful man had he remained in Ur of the Chaldees, but he would not have become a *mature* man, a *fulfilled* man in the will of God.

The example given in Hebrews, to warn us against going back into the old life, is that of the nation of Israel. Whenever a new trial or difficulty appeared on their journey from Egypt to Canaan, the people usually responded by (a) complaining, and (b) expressing a desire to go back to Egypt. It seems incredible that they remembered the food and forgot the bondage! "We remember the fish which we used to eat free in Egypt . . ." (Numbers 11:5). Free, indeed! They paid a dear price for the fish, the cucumbers, the melons, the leeks, the onions, and the garlic!

The person who thinks of "going back to Egypt" when life gets tough is really admitting that he has a "hidden agenda" in his heart. Plan A is to obey God, so long as life is comfortable. Plan B is to go back to the old life when things get uncomfortable. The tragedy is that *neither plan ever succeeds.* Plan A is defeated by the hidden agenda of Plan B in the heart. Instead of allowing that generation of Jews to go back go Egypt, God kept them wandering in the wilderness until they all died. They would not have been satisfied in Egypt, and it would have disgraced His name to send them there; but they really were not ready for Canaan. So, they participated for forty years in the world's longest funeral march. You could follow their route: it was marked by graves.

You could follow Abraham's route as well: it was marked by altars. Wherever he went, Abraham pitched his tent and built his altar. The tent was moved; the altar remained. The tent told everybody that Abraham was not a citizen of this world; the altar announced that he was a citizen of heaven. It is not enough to be detached from earth; we must be attached to heaven. Nobody would believe Abraham was really God's pilgrim were it not for the dual testimony of the tent and the altar, separation and sacrifice, walk and worship, the changing scene and the unchanging fellowship. The tent without the altar would be folly; the altar without the tent would be hypocrisy.

Yes, if the patriarchs had been thinking about the country from which they came out, they would have had opportunity to return; but returning to their past was the farthest thing from their thoughts. "Beware lest you take my son back there!" Abraham warned his steward (Genesis 24:6). When you have "tasted the good word of God and the powers of the age to come" (Hebrews 6:5), you lose your taste for the cucumbers, melons, leeks, onions, and garlic. Egypt simply has nothing to offer.

Abraham built his altar; he was not ashamed to call God *his* God. And God was not ashamed to be called "The God of Abraham." "For those who honor Me I will honor" (1 Samuel 2:30). This is not a commercial arrangement by which God secures our worship because He blesses us. That was Satan's interpretation of things when he accused Job. No, God does not honor us because we have earned it, but because we can be trusted with it. God does not indiscriminately attach His name to a man. We never read in the Bible, "The God of Lot" or "The God of Esau," because God could never share His name with men like Lot and Esau.

Because Abraham and Sarah had dedicated hearts, the desires of their hearts were godly, not selfish. True, they made their mistakes and had their days of doubt and disobedience; but *the bent of their lives* was heavenly. There was no hidden agenda, no Plan B. When you delight yourself in the Lord, then He delights in you, and He plans for you the things that will satisfy the desires of your heart *because those desires delight Him.*

Here, then, are the marks of the true pilgrim—and you cannot have one without the others, if you are going to move ahead and claim your inheritance.

Open ears. "Speak, for Thy servant is listening" (1 Samuel 3:10).

Obedient feet. "Faith without works is dead" (James 2:26).

Steady eyes. "Fixing our eyes on Jesus, the author and perfecter of faith . . ." (Hebrews 12:2).

Ready lips. "Therefore do not be ashamed of the testimony of our Lord . . ." (2 Timothy 1:8).

Dedicated heart. "Do you love Me more than these?" (John 21:15).

Abraham was seventy-five years old when he abandoned Ur of the Chaldees and ventured out to establish a new home, with no forwarding address.

We are never too old to become God's pilgrims.

Don't delay!

And don't look back!

6/ ABRAHAM AND SARAH: TWO RESURRECTIONS
HEBREWS 11:11, 12, 17–19

The central theme that runs through these verses is God's resurrection power in the lives of believing people. Abraham and Sarah were as good as dead, yet God enabled them to have a son. Issac was as good as dead when Abraham put him on the altar, yet "symbolically" he was raised from the dead.

Do you need to experience this kind of power? Well, if you don't, I certainly do—and most of the Christians I know are also in need of God's resurrection power. The demands that life makes upon us today are too great for us to handle alone. We all need to experience "the power of His [Christ's] resurrection" (Philippians 3:10), power that is "able to do exceeding abundantly beyond all that we ask or think" (Ephesians 3:20, 21). This power is available to those who will believe God's promises and act upon them.

The key factor, of course, is faith. These verses record two experiences of faith in the life of Abraham and Sarah.

1. FAITH TO RECEIVE THE BLESSING
(Hebrews 11:11, 12).

Sarah is one of two women named in Hebrews 11; the
other is Rahab (v. 31). What a contrast there is between
these two women! Sarah was a member of the chosen
Jewish race, while Rahab was a Gentile, an outsider (see
Ephesians 2:11ff.). Sarah was called out of a condemned
city, but Rahab remained in the city of Jericho and was
saved along with her family. Sarah was a virtuous woman,
but Rahab was a harlot. Yet both of them shared in the
blessing of God *because they had faith.* Both of them had
to depend wholly on the sovereign grace of God.

Even though we must trust Christ and be saved as
individuals, faith is a family affair. Noah's faith involved
his whole family, and Abraham's experience of faith
involved his wife. They were fellow-heirs of the grace of
life (1 Peter 3:7). God could not have fulfilled his promise
through Abraham alone; He also needed Sarah.

But when you read the record, you wonder what kind
of faith Sarah really had! In Genesis 16, Sarah suggested
that Abraham marry her maid, Hagar, and have a son by
her. When the son, Ishmael, was conceived, Sarah then
turned upon both her maid and her husband! When
unbelief tries to solve a problem, it always causes a
greater problem.

Then, when God did announce that Sarah, not Hagar,
was to be the mother of the promised heir, *Sarah laughed
at the announcement!* (See Genesis 18:9-15.) She tried to
lie her way out of it, but the Lord knew what she had
done, and He rebuked her for it; *but He did not alter
either His plan or His promise.* "If we are faithless, He
remains faithful; for He cannot deny Himself" (2 Timothy
2:13).

On a scale of one to ten, Sarah's faith would seem to
rate a zero; yet here she is, listed in Hebrews 11. And
none of her mistakes is even mentioned! But, remember,
Hebrews 11 is a record of *faith,* not unbelief; it lists the
victories, not the defeats. This is a great encouragement

to me, because I have more than once tried to second-guess God, improve on His plans, and hasten the fulfillment of His promises. But God is not keeping a record of the failures of our faith so that He can rebuke us. Rather, He is keeping a record of the victories of our faith so that He can reward us.

Sarah's lapse of faith in Genesis 16, and her laughter of unbelief in Genesis 18, were but *incidents* in a life that generally was marked by faith and obedience. Let the reader who is without sin cast the first stone. God has categorized these incidents along with Moses' temper explosion, David's adultery, Peter's denial of Christ, and Thomas' unbelief—and has forgotten them all. "And their sins and their lawless deeds I will remember no more" (Hebrews 10:17).

Reading Christian biography has been a hobby of mine since I was a seminary student. Some biographies read like press releases. They so magnify the perfections of the subject of the book, you wonder as you read whether the person ever made a mistake, broke a promise, or displayed unchristian behavior. On the other hand, there are some biographies that major on the warts. The writer is out to "smash the image" of some honored person, and so he dredges up (or manufactures) as much historical mud as he can.

The Bible does neither. It tells us the truth about people, warts and all, so that through them we might learn the truth about ourselves and God. The sins of the saints, recorded in the Bible, all remind us that God *in His grace* can forgive us, but that God *in His government* must permit us to reap what we have sown. The record does not encourage us to sin; but it does encourage us, if we have sinned, to trust God to forgive and to work out His will.

The parallel passage to Hebrews 11:11, 12 is Romans 4:13-25, and it should be studied carefully. The emphasis in Romans is on Abraham, while in Hebrews it is on Sarah.

Both Abraham and Sarah were "as good as dead" as far as begetting or bearing children. Sarah was sixty-five years old, and Abraham seventy-five, when God first gave the promise that He would make of them a great nation (Genesis 12:2). They waited for ten years and still no son was born. When Abraham was eighty-five, he fell in with Sarah's "Plan B" (the hidden agenda) and married Hagar; and when he was eighty-six, he was given a son, Ishmael (Genesis 16:3, 16). We read nothing more about Abraham and Sarah *for thirteen years!* Unbelief always results in silence.

When Abraham was ninety-nine, and Sarah eighty-nine, the Lord again spoke to him and reaffirmed the promise of a son; and this time He made it very clear that Sarah was to be the mother (Genesis 17:15-17). But what about Ishmael, who for thirteen years had woven himself into the fabric of the home? "Oh that Ishmael might live before Thee!" (Genesis 17:18). Faith and unbelief, the future and the past, the spiritual and the natural, were struggling in Abraham's heart. Until you have known these struggles personally, don't be too hard on the old man.

We have noted before that God's power is released through God's promises, when you and I exercise faith. God had promised that one man would have descendants as numerous as the stars in the heavens and the grains of sand on the seashore (Genesis 15:5; 22:17), and He later repeated this promise to Isaac (26:4) and Jacob (32:12). One man become a multitude—and a man "as good as dead" at that? Impossible! "With men this is impossible, but with God all things are possible" (Matthew 19:26).

The link between God's power and man's poverty is *God's promise.* Sarah and Abraham "considered Him faithful who had promised" (11:11).

Saturday, September 4, 1869, ought to be marked on our calendars as a red-letter day in the history of the Church; for on that day, one of her greatest sons entered into a new life of peace and power. On that day, missionary J. Hudson Taylor read a letter from a fellow missionary to China, John McCarthy, and discovered "the exchanged life." Among other things, McCarthy wrote:

Abiding, not striving nor struggling; looking off unto Him; trusting Him for present power. . . . Not a striving to have faith . . . but a looking off to the Faithful One seems all we need; a resting in the Loved One entirely, for time and for eternity.

Later, Hudson Taylor recalled, "As I read, I saw it all! I looked to Jesus, and when I saw—oh, how joy flowed!" His fellow missionaries saw a dramatic change in his life. He worked just as hard, but it was joyful ministry, not burdensome toil. He seemed to be drawing upon limitless stores of strength and power, hidden resources from heaven. God blessed his life and work in a singular way, and God received the glory.

Hudson Taylor learned the same secret that Abraham and Sarah shared: "Not a striving to have faith . . . but a looking off to the Faithful One." Paul expressed it this way: "And being fully assured that what He had promised, He was able also to perform" (Romans 4:21). God's power is stored in His promises, and that power is released when you and I believe God. Abraham and Sarah didn't look at their own "dead" bodies, but to the living God "who gives life to the dead and calls into being that which does not exist" (Romans 4:17).

Too many of us are prone to trust ourselves, or even to trust our faith, instead of trusting the Faithful One. We can fail, and our faith can fail, but "not one word has failed of all His good promise" (1 Kings 8:56). The promise of God is faithful because the God of the promise is faithful.

In what area of your life do you desperately need to experience Christ's resurrection power? Find a promise that relates to that area, focus it on the need, and by faith claim the promise—and resurrection power will go to work! Look by faith to the Faithful One whose promises never fail!

2. FAITH TO SURRENDER THE BLESSING (Hebrews 11:17-19).

"In the commencement of the spiritual life," wrote Madame Guyon, "our hardest task is to bear with our neighbor; in its progress, with ourselves; and in its end, with God."

Abraham began his life of faith not knowing *where*. God told him he would have a son, but Abraham did not know *when* or *how*. Then God told him that his destination was Canaan; and, twenty-four years later, he told him that Sarah would bear a son the next year. God kept His promise, as He always does, and the son was born.

But fulfilled promises, like answered prayers, can be dangerous. We may get more involved in the gift than the Giver, and this kind of attitude transforms a blessing into a burden—and then into an idol. One of the most ominous warnings in Scripture is found in Malachi 2:2.

"If you do not listen, and if you do not take it to heart to give honor to My name," says the Lord of hosts, "then I will send the curse upon you, and I will curse your blessings; and indeed, I have cursed them already, because you are not taking it to heart."

If you are going to live by faith, then expect your faith to be tested. A faith that can't be tested can't be trusted. Not all the difficult experiences of life are tests from God. The family problems caused by Ishmael were not a special test; they were simply the sad consequences of following Plan B. Abraham's conflict with his neighbors over water rights was but one of the many problems people experience when they have to live together.

Nor should we blame the devil for the tests of life. The devil *tempts* us to bring out the worst in us, but the Father *tests* us to bring out the best in us. James 1:12-16 makes it clear that temptations arise *within us*, while testings come from *above us*, sent by the Father of lights. Temptations seem reasonable; in fact, it is the logic of temptation that makes it so dangerous. From "You will be like God!" to "All these things will I give You, if You fall down and worship me!"—Satan's offers all appear to be reasonable and impossible to refuse. But God's tests seem unreasonable, even ungodly! They defy explanation.

Temptation comes to all believers (1 Corinthians 10:13), but tests (such as the one Abraham and Isaac experienced) come only to seasoned saints. God didn't have to test Lot; Sodom took care of that. The fact that Abraham was tested in this way was in reality an honor, a Pulitzer Prize in "The School of Faith." Temptations are pretty much standardized, but divine tests are tailor-made for each servant of God. They are special because each child of God is special to the Father.

If you and I had been planning the test recorded in Genesis 22, we never would have asked for Isaac. We would have asked Abraham to give up Ishmael. After all, Ishmael was a mistake, the child of unbelief and flesh, not faith and Spirit. Here are two sons, Ishmael and Isaac. The one reminds Abraham of the defeat of unbelief, while the other bears witness to the victory of faith. One embodies problems; the other embodies promise. Certainly Abraham loved Ishmael, his firstborn son; yet God did not ask for Ishmael on the altar. He asked for Isaac.

Why?

Because everything important to Abraham was wrapped up in Isaac. To begin with, Abraham's *faith* was certainly involved in Isaac. Abraham believed God's promise, that he would have a multitude of descendants, and that his seed would bring blessing to the whole world. If Isaac died, what happened to God's promise? All of Abraham's *hope* was wrapped up in Isaac. The future of the nation—indeed, the future of the world—depended on Isaac. If Isaac died, who would build the nation of Israel?

There is no question that Abraham's *love* bound him to his son as perhaps no father and son have ever been bound. "Take now your son, your only son, whom you love . . ." (Genesis 22:2).

This was not the first time Abraham's faith had been tested by God. No sooner had the patriarch arrived in Canaan than he faced a famine, a serious situation for a man who lived off of his flocks and herds. Abraham failed that test by rushing down to Egypt. No sooner did he return to Bethel than he got involved in a family quarrel with his nephew Lot. There just wasn't enough room for all their flocks and herds, and somebody had to give in. Abraham passed that test and God honored him for it.

After the famine test and the flock test came the fortune test (Genesis 14:17-24). The evil king of Sodom offered to make Abraham rich. But Abraham passed that test with flying colors; in fact, he won it *before the battle* (14:22). His next test was the family test, the problem with Sarah, Hagar, and Ishmael; and Abraham failed.

But none of these tests could compare with the test recorded in Genesis 22, though they helped to prepare Abraham for it. Over the years, Abraham was learning more about himself, his faith, and his God. Trials are a refining process that should leave us with a purer faith (1 Peter 1:7). Trials help to develop the kind of character that God can bless and use (James 1:1-4). Each trial that we endure by faith brings us closer to God and makes us more like Him. Each victory of faith also prepares us for the next test.

The principle, then, is this: if we don't give our blessings back to God, they will turn into cursings. Ishmael was a curse that Abraham wanted God to turn into a blessing. Isaac was a blessing that was in danger of being turned into a curse *if Abraham refused to put him on the altar.* Jesus taught this same principle: "For whoever wishes to save his life shall lose it; but whoever loses his life for My sake shall find it" (Matthew 16:25).

Contrary to what you see in Bible storybooks, Isaac was not a little boy when God told his father to put him on the altar. He was a young man, and the longer he had been in the home, the deeper was his father's love for him. And yet, when Abraham heard the command of God, he didn't pray, "Oh, that Isaac might live before You!" He didn't pamper Isaac or protect Isaac. Immediately, Abraham obeyed the voice of God. Most of us would have seized upon every reason (or excuse) for delay, but not Abraham. Faith does not look for escapes, or ask for explanations; it simply obeys and leaves the rest with God.

It was Abraham's faith that carried him through this test. Not faith in himself, or faith in his faith, but faith in the promise of God. What promise? "In Isaac your descendants shall be called" (Hebrews 11:18; Genesis 21:12).

What did Abraham do with this promise? Hebrews 11:19 tells us that "He considered." The word translated "considered" means "to reckon, to take into account, to calculate." It gives us our English words "logic" and "logistics." While faith seems contrary to reason, there is a reasoning that grows out of faith.

"If God intends for Isaac to have descendants," Abraham reasoned, "then Isaac cannot die. This means that either God will stop me from slaying him, or, if I slay him, God will raise him from the dead."

The more you contemplate it, the more wonderful Abraham's faith becomes. As far as we know, he had never seen anybody raised from the dead. But he and Sarah had experienced God's resurrection power in their own lives! There was no reason why God could not perform the same miracle in Isaac's dead body. And so

Abraham went "from faith to faith" (Romans 1:17) as he walked with God.

"Stay here with the donkey," the old man said to his two servants, "and I and the lad will go yonder; and we will worship and return to you" (Genesis 22:5). Note the plural pronoun: "we will worship and return to you." Abraham was bearing witness to others of the resurrection power of God, even though they didn't understand it. But think of what that word meant to Isaac. His loving father had assured him that the altar was not the end of his life, but the beginning!

Unless you and I give our blessings back to God, they will only remain to curse us. Why is this so? Because unless we experience death, burial, and resurrection, we cannot multiply and be a blessing to the whole world. Listen to the words of Jesus:

"Truly, truly, I say to you, unless a grain of wheat falls into the earth and dies, it remains by itself alone; but if it dies, it bears much fruit. He who loves his life loses it; and he who hates his life in this world shall keep it to life eternal." John 12:24, 25

It was God's desire that Isaac be a blessing to the whole world. Isaac was certainly a blessing to Abraham and Sarah, but that was not enough. *Our blessings turn into curses when we keep them to ourselves and use them only for our own enjoyment.* We forget that God gave them to us to be shared. Every blessing from God is both an ending and a beginning. If we love the blessing and keep it to ourselves, we will lose it, and the world will lose as well. But if we love God and give the blessing back to Him, we will keep it; but at the same time, we will bless others.

Jesus illustrated this truth with a seed. Protect the seed and it remains fruitless and alone. Plant the seed and it becomes fruitful and multiplies. Death, burial, resurrection. Even our Lord had to experience these things in order to bring salvation to a lost world. Blessings held in the hand are limited and are potential curses. Blessings placed on the altar are unlimited and have a potential for enriching a whole world.

This explains why we lose what we keep and gain what we give. It also explains why "It is more blessed to give than to receive" (Acts 20:35).

But all of this requires faith! It is not a mere commercial transaction between us and God. It is rather the result of a living relationship, a trust, a desire to please and glorify Him. We must never get the idea that Abraham's faith made it *easy* for him to bind his son and put him on the altar. His paternal affections were normal and his emotions were real. Our greatest battles are not waged between love and hatred, but between two loves: our love for God and our love for God's blessings. And the deeper we love, the more difficult is the test.

How much easier it would have been to put Ishmael on the altar! But Ishmael represented the past, and Isaac the future. It takes little faith to yield our past to God. For one thing, we already know what it is; and for another, it is probably littered with failures just like Ishmael's. What kind of loving faith would give God that kind of sacrifice? "For I will not offer burnt offerings to the Lord my God which cost me nothing" (2 Samuel 24:24).

So, when Abraham put Isaac on the altar, he was giving to God all that he had—his faith, his hope, his love. Abraham's heart belonged to the Giver, not to the gift. As a result, Isaac experienced death, burial, and resurrection, *but he was not alone or unfruitful!* Instead of being a blessing only to Abraham and Sarah, Isaac became a blessing to the whole world!

Because Abraham opened his heart to believe, and opened his hand to give, God opened his eyes to see. Yes, he saw a ram, caught in a thicket; but he saw much more. Up until now, his eyes of faith had seen the heavenly country and the heavenly city, but now he saw *the Son of God!* "Your father Abraham rejoiced to see My day," said Jesus to the Jews, "and he saw it and was glad" (John 8:56). Abraham saw Jesus Christ when he received his son back "as a type."

Isaac, then, is a type of Jesus Christ, the Obedient Son. He is one of the many Old Testament "pictures" of the Savior. When you read Genesis 22 in this light, it takes on new meaning.

You see the Father and the Son together, bound by love, each willing to give. "So the two of them walked on together" (Genesis 22:6, 8). The first time you find the word "love" in the Bible, it is in Genesis 22:2: "Take now your son, your only son, whom you love. . . ." We read that and then remember John 5:20, "For the Father loves the Son. . . ." We are so accustomed to quoting "For God so loved the world" (John 3:16) that we forget that the Father loved the Son long before there was a world.

Isaac asked, "Where is the lamb?" The answer came centuries later from the lips of John the Baptist: "Behold, the Lamb of God who takes away the sin of the world!" (John 1:29). That explains the burden on Isaac's back, wood fit only for the fire. That also explains the knife and the fire. "The wages of sin is death" (Romans 6:23). "For our God is a consuming fire" (Hebrews 12:29).

In the heart of Abraham, and in the sight of God, Isaac died; but in reality, he was delivered by a substitute. The ram died in his place. But nobody took Jesus' place *because nobody could.* He was the sinless, spotless Lamb of God, the only one who could bear the sins of the world on His body and grant us forgiveness. "And there is salvation in no one else," Peter declared to the Jewish council, "for there is no other name under heaven that has been given among men, by which we must be saved" (Acts 4:12).

All of this Abraham saw through the eyes of faith, and because he saw it, he was glad. He named that place on the mountain "Jehovah-jireh," which means "The Lord

will see to it, the Lord will provide." Will provide *what?*
*Whatever you need in order to turn your testing into
triumph!* In Abraham's case, God *immediately* provided
a ram, and *ultimately* He provided His own Son.

Each test we experience involves both the immediate
and the ultimate. We must take care that the immediate
provision doesn't distract us from the ultimate Person,
Jesus Christ. If that happens, our victory becomes defeat
and the blessing will turn into a curse. At each place of
testing, at each altar, we must be able to say "Jehovah-
jireh!" and mean it. "In the mount of the Lord it will be
provided, it will be seen!"

Because Abraham was a loving father, the test reached
to the depths of his heart; but because he was a believing
pilgrim, he passed the test victoriously. He still had eyes
that could see the glory of God and ears that could hear
the voice of God. "I will greatly bless you," said God,
"and I will greatly multiply your seed" (Genesis 22:17).
Was it worth it all? Of course it was! "And in your seed all
the nations of the earth shall be blessed, because you
have obeyed My voice" (Genesis 22:18). The seed was not
fruitless and alone! Because it was buried and raised
from the dead, it would multiply and bless the whole
world!

When Abraham explained his plans to the two young
men who accompanied him and Isaac, he used a remarkable word. It is the word *worship.* "I and the lad will go
yonder; and we will worship . . ." (Genesis 22:5). *Faith
transforms an experience of painful sacrifice into an
experience of worship.* Isaac became a "living sacrifice"
(see Romans 12:1) to the glory of God. He typifies our
Lord Jesus Christ who in heaven today is "a living sacrifice," still bearing the wounds of Calvary.

What greater honor could God bestow upon Isaac than
to make him like the Lord Jesus Christ?

Every life has an "Isaac" that must be put on the altar. It is
not a bad thing; it is a good thing, a blessing from the

hand of God. It might even be an answer to prayer, the fulfillment of God's promise. It is a source of joy, something (or someone) for whom we give God thanks every single day.

But this blessing was given to us *to be shared,* not to be sheltered. If we keep it to ourselves, it will cease to be a blessing and will become a curse. If we give it to God, as difficult as the experience may be, it will remain a blessing and will be used by God to bless the whole world. The seed must be planted and die before it can bear fruit.

It takes faith to *receive* the blessing, but it also takes faith to *surrender* the blessing. Three words in Hebrews 11:19 point the way to victory: "God is able."

"And being fully assured that what He had promised, He was able also to perform" (Romans 4:21).

God is able! But His ability, great as it is, must be claimed by our faith. The Savior still asks us, "Do you believe that I am able to do this?" (Matthew 9:28).

Perhaps many of us are answering, "I do believe; help my unbelief" (Mark 9:24).

Whatever that "Isaac" is in your life, put it on the altar. Until it becomes a "living sacrifice," it can never bless the world. As long as it blesses you only, it is an idol, and it will become a curse. The moment it is yielded, it starts to bless others to the glory of God.

The resurrection of Jesus Christ proves that "God is able."

Now to Him who is able to do exceeding abundantly beyond all that we ask or think, according to the power that works within us, to Him be the glory in the church and in Christ Jesus to all generations forever and ever.
Ephesians 3:20, 21

By faith, receive the blessing He wants to give you.

By faith, give that blessing back to Him, and start to be a blessing to the whole world, "to all generations forever and ever"!

7/ ISAAC, JACOB, JOSEPH: FAITH FOR THE FUTURE
HEBREWS 11:20–22

Isaac, Jacob, Joseph: it would be difficult to find three
men more different from each other and yet still related.
Isaac was the son of a famous father and the father of a
famous son; yet his own life seems rather ordinary—except, of course, for the altar experience recorded in
Genesis 22. He had a remarkable birth; but beyond that,
Isaac seems like Mr. Average Citizen.

Not so with Jacob! Here you meet the master schemer,
the manipulator of men and events. At birth, he grabbed
his twin brother by the heel, and then spent the rest of
his life trying to trip anybody who hindered his plans.
He saw visions; he wrestled with God; he produced a big
family; he died in peace after a lifetime of war. You would
never believe that Jacob came from the loins of Isaac.

Of Joseph, you can say only good things. No matter
what page of his biography you read, he shows up as the
knight in shining armor. Persecuted by his brothers, he
still refused to carry a grudge and seek revenge. Tempted
to defile himself, he fled lest he sin against God. Forced
to serve when he was destined to rule, he patiently
waited and trusted that his dreams would not become

nightmares. Is Joseph the son of Jacob? Where did this young man get his integrity?

As different as they are from one another, these three men are all men of faith. That in itself qualifies them to run the race along with the other men and women included in Hebrews 11. The tie that binds them together here is the faith they evidenced, especially in their last days. They had faith for the future, the kind of faith that even death could not weaken or destroy. "All these died in faith" (11:13); but before they died, they confessed their faith either by conferring a blessing on others or by asking a favor from others. Their faith pointed to "things to come."

1. ISAAC: THE FUTURE BLESSING (Hebrews 11:20). The story is found in Genesis 27. It is the saga of a family that is about to self-destruct: Isaac, the father; Rebekah, the mother; Esau, the older son; Jacob, the younger son. It is a story of greed, treachery, deception, and favoritism; and yet this was once an exemplary family. When you consider the actors in this drama, you wonder that there was any blessing at all!

Isaac was *a declining father.* There was a time when he had been a spiritual giant. After all, had he not agreed to be put on the altar as a sacrifice to God? Had he not trusted God to give him the right wife, and he and his wife prayed earnestly for a family? Had he not faithfully pitched his tent and built his altars, just as Abraham had done before him?

Yes, all of these things were true. But in spite of them, Isaac was not at his best spiritually. He knew that Jacob was ordained of God to receive the patriarchal blessing (Genesis 25:21-23), *yet he tried to give it to Esau!* It was no secret that Esau was his favorite of the two boys. So often a quiet meditative man like Isaac admires the man of the field, the hunter, a man such as Esau. Isaac was blind physically but even more blind spiritually. He was deliberately trying to disobey God.

But Isaac was no match for Rebekah, *the deceiving mother.* She knew her husband's plot, but she also knew her husband's weakness: he had to depend on his senses. So she dressed Jacob up to impersonate Esau, and the trick worked. Isaac *did* trust his senses: he *felt* the hairy hands (27:21), *smelled* the out-of-doors fragrance of the garments (v. 27), and *tasted* the delicious meal (v. 25). His only suspicion related to the voice: it sounded like Jacob, not Esau (v. 22). But when a person lives by his senses, and leaves God out, he can easily be mistaken about one little piece of evidence.

So Rebekah turned her son Jacob into a hypocrite, a schemer; and a schemer he remained for almost the rest of his years. He not only schemed, but he was schemed against. Rebekah hoped to send Jacob away for a short visit, and then the family could welcome him home; but she never saw her favorite son again. Esau threatened to kill his brother, and he would have if Jacob had stayed home.

God overruled Isaac's disobedience and arranged for Jacob to receive his rightful blessing. God permitted Rebekah and Jacob to accomplish this end, but He did not approve the means. Men and women of faith should never do evil that good may come (Romans 6:15). If we trust God for the end, we also must trust Him for the means to the end. Rebekah was simply following the bad example of her mother-in-law, Sarah, who had used Hagar to try to help God keep His promise. In both cases, the families suffered the sad consequences.

Since Esau was the firstborn, he should have had both the birthright and the blessing; but he sold the birthright (Genesis 25:29-34) and lost the blessing. But God had determined already that Jacob, not Esau, would be treated as the firstborn, and therefore receive the blessing. Esau

is a picture of the "natural man," clever, successful,
self-sufficient, liked by his neighbors, physically attractive, courageous, a man with everything but faith. From
the human point of view, Esau would have been everybody's choice for the blessing; but God had other plans.
As we shall discover in verse 23, God often set aside the
firstborn and chose the second-born.

This blessing was not simply a family formality, the
aged father conveying "best wishes and glorious hopes"
as he put his shaking hands upon the head of his son.
No, the blessing was very real; it was not just so many
pious words that disappeared into the air and became
happy memories. It was not just the father's blessing; it
was *God's* blessing. It guaranteed to Jacob "the dew of
heaven, and of the fatness of the earth, and an abundance
of grain and new wine" (Genesis 27:28). It assured him
victory over his enemies and preeminence over his
brothers and sisters. It linked him with the blessings God
promised Abraham!

No wonder Esau wept when he discovered what he
had lost! And no wonder Isaac trembled when he discovered it was Jacob, not his beloved Esau, who received the
blessing (Genesis 28:33). God could have brought all of
this about in a true and proper manner; but when He is
not permitted to rule, then He must overrule. The blessing of God is linked to the sovereign will of God, and that
will must always prevail.

So many irritating problems nudge at your mind and
heart when you consider this event. How could God
actually bless Jacob when he was part of such a degrading
masquerade? How could God bless *through* Isaac when
he was deliberately trying to overrule the sovereign
choice of God? The whole atmosphere of the home was
contrary to any kind of blessing, yet God did bless Jacob.
"Where sin increased, grace abounded all the more"
(Romans 5:20).

But Isaac did bless Esau as well! The despairing man

tried to get his father to change his mind, but this was not possible (see Hebrews 12: 16, 17). Jacob had received the blessing and it could not be revoked. "Yes, and he shall be blessed" (Genesis 27:33). But the blessing Esau received was far different from Jacob's. Esau's dwelling would be *away from* everything God had given Jacob. There would be no guaranteed defense from God; he would have to live by the sword. About the only hope Isaac gave his favorite son was that he would one day get rid of Jacob's yoke. But what good is freedom if you have nothing to enjoy? Jacob had the luxuries, and Esau barely had the necessities.

As the possessor of both the birthright and the blessing, Jacob was a wealthy man. God in His grace had honored him, but God in His government had to discipline him. Before Jacob could enjoy the fatness, he had to endure some bitterness; and before his enemies could bow down before him, he himself had to learn to serve. His own sons deceived him just the way he had deceived his father. He suffered deception and deprivation under the hand of Laban, his scheming father-in-law. Even *with* the blessing, life was not easy for Jacob; yet, in the end, he prevailed.

It remains only to note that One Greater than Isaac has already blessed His people "with every spiritual blessing in the heavenly places" (Ephesians 1:3). *And we shall be blessed!* Our future is secure and we have sufficient for the present. The present blessing guarantees the future blessing. What more could we ask?

2. JACOB: THE FUTURE INHERITANCE (Hebrews 11:21).

The blessed now becomes the blesser, and this is as it should be. After all, God originally blessed Abraham so that, through him, all the world would be blessed. We are to be channels, not reservoirs.

The scene is recorded in Genesis 48, and one of the key words in that chapter is "bless." Jacob confessed that all that he ever had or did was the result of the blessing of God (48:2-8). Jacob then blessed Joseph (48:15, 16) and Joseph's two sons, Ephraim and Manasseh (48:20). A tender scene indeed, with the aged father, the loving son, and the embarrassed grandsons. How long would they have to listen to the old man talk about the good old days? Little did they realize the impact that those trembling lips and shaking hands would have on their future!

Years before, Jacob's aged father, a dying man, had blessed two sons and had reversed their order. They were born *Esau and Jacob,* but they were blessed *Jacob and Esau.* Now Jacob was to do the same thing with Joseph's two sons. Until that hour, the boys were known as *Manasseh and Ephraim;* but after that hour, it would be *Ephraim and Manasseh.* This was really nothing new: Cain, the firstborn, had been set aside for Abel; and Ishmael, Abraham's firstborn, was rejected to make room for Isaac. "However, the spiritual is not first, but the natural; then the spiritual" (1 Corinthians 15:46). Our Lord was amazed that scholarly Nicodemus had not seen this truth in the Old Testament and, as a result, didn't understand the meaning of the second birth. When will sinners, even *religious* sinners, realize that our first birth is not sufficient for God to accept us? "That which is born of the flesh is flesh; and that which is born of the Spirit is spirit," said our Lord. "Do not marvel that I said to you, 'You must be born again' " (John 3:6, 7).

Joseph was upset with his father when the old man put his right hand on Ephraim and his left hand on Manasseh. This is the only recorded imperfection in Joseph's otherwise blameless life. But Jacob knew what he was doing, and he explained that he was adopting Joseph's two sons and guaranteeing that the younger of the two would receive the patriarchal blessing. Ephraim and Manasseh were replacing Jacob's first two sons, Reuben and Simeon. In a sense, Jacob was making Joseph his firstborn, and was settling final accounts with his father-in-law, Laban.

You see, Laban had tricked Jacob on Jacob's wedding night, and had given him Leah for a wife instead of the promised Rachel. That meant that Jacob had to labor seven more years to get the woman he really loved. Rachel may have had the beauty, but it was Leah who had the babies: Reuben, Simeon, Levi, Judah, Issachar, and Zebulun, and, for good measure, a daughter named Dinah. Rachel bore Jacob only two sons, Joseph and Benjamin, and she died giving birth to Benjamin.

So Jacob replaced Leah's firstborn with Rachel's firstborn! Both Reuben and Simeon had been guilty of gross sins. Reuben had lain with Bilhah, Jacob's concubine (Genesis 35:22; 49:3, 4). Simeon had lied to the people of Shechem and then, along with his brother Levi, had murdered the men (Genesis 34; 49:5-7). The sad record of Reuben's sin is even recorded in the official genealogy (1 Chronicles 5:1). It took many years for Reuben's sin to catch up with him, but catch up with him it did. There were 59,300 men of war in the tribe of Simeon when the nation left Egypt (Numbers 1:23), but only 22,200 when the new generation was counted (Numbers 26:14). Simeon was actually absorbed into the tribe of Judah (Joshua 19:1-9), while Reuben was given land on the other side of Jordan.

But let's not lose the spiritual lesson that Jacob is teaching us: when we deliberately sin, we endanger our inheritance. "For this you know with certainty, that no immoral or impure person . . . has an inheritance in the kingdom of Christ and God" (Ephesians 5:5). Reuben and Simeon jeopardized their own future, and the future inheritance of their descendants, by their sins of lust, deception, and murder. Simeon's descendants just seemed to dwindle, and Reuben's tribe played no important role in the history of the nation. What a tragedy when the firstborn and second-born forfeit the blessings of the future for the pleasures of the present!

What gave Jacob the right to defy nature and reverse the positions of the two boys?

The Cross of Jesus Christ.

Jacob *crossed his hands* when he deliberately placed his right hand on Ephraim and his left hand on Manasseh. Only the Cross of Jesus Christ can set aside your first birth and establish a second birth. "And as Moses lifted up the serpent in the wilderness, even so must the Son of Man be lifted up; that whoever believes may in Him have eternal life" (John 3:14, 15).

Human nature cannot reverse human nature. Fallen human nature is a part of the problem, not a part of the answer. Deliverance can come only from above. The sinner must be born again, and (paradoxical as it seems) that birth can come only out of death, the death of the Savior. The Cross has set aside the first and established the second. First the natural, then the spiritual.

There was more than birth involved in the blessing; there was also growth and fruitfulness. The tribe of Ephraim extended from the Mediterranean Sea to the Jordan River, right across the middle of the land. Even though it had lost numbers between the two censuses (from 40,500 to 32,000), it grew and prospered. Joseph, indeed, did become a "fruitful bough" by means of his two sons (Genesis 49:22).

But there was even more: Jacob invoked a *spiritual* blessing on the lads, as he was blessing their father (48:15, 16). What a testimony these words are to the faithfulness of God on the lips of a man who was prone to manage life his own way! God had been his Shepherd and Redeemer: He had guided him and guarded him all the days of his life. Jacob was not ashamed to confess his faith in God, and God was not ashamed to be called "the God of Jacob."

Jacob's posture and attitude are mentioned: "he . . . worshiped, leaning on the top of his staff" (Hebrews 11:21). About all he had brought from home, that day he fled for his life, were his father's blessing and his own staff (Genesis 32:10). That staff was the symbol of his life: he was a pilgrim. Abraham had his tent and his altar; Isaac had his tent and his wells; Jacob had his tent and his staff.

The staff was a reminder to Jacob that God had blessed him. "I am unworthy of all the lovingkindness and of all the faithfulness which Thou hast shown to Thy servant," he had prayed when he heard Esau was coming to meet him. "For with my staff only I crossed this Jordan, and now I have become two companies" (Genesis 32:10). It was also a reminder that God had broken him; for after wrestling all night with the Lord, Jacob *limped* back into camp, a new man with a new name.

Jacob was a pilgrim to the very end. "All these died in faith" (Hebrews 11:13). Death presented no fears to Jacob. The God who had shepherded him all his life would take him into eternity. "For such is God, our God forever and ever; He will guide us until death" (Psalm 48:14). And then what? "With Thy counsel Thou wilt guide me, and afterward receive me to glory" (Psalm 73:24). Jacob would not need his staff when he walked through the valley. "For Thou art with me; Thy rod and Thy staff, they comfort me" (Psalm 23:4).

Yes, Jacob died like a true pilgrim, leaning on his staff. But he also died like a prince: "Israel . . . you have striven with God and with men and have prevailed" (Genesis 32:28). He turned that deathbed into a throne as he conferred the blessing on Joseph and his sons. Jacob had wrestled with God and with himself; and God had given him the victory. He was now a God-controlled man. There would be no more scheming, no more manipulating of people, no more trying to second-guess God. It was not that he was "too old" for such things; it was that he was too wise, too mature. God had finally prevailed.

Jacob worshiped God and blessed his grandsons. What a way to die! There was worship in his heart, blessing on his lips, and power in his hands! Instead of looking back and remembering all of his failures—and there had been many!—he looked ahead at what God would do through Ephraim and Manasseh. He looked up and asked God to give one more blessing, and God answered his prayer. Isaac's faith centered on the future blessing, and now Jacob was sharing that blessing as he focused on the future inheritance.

3. JOSEPH: THE FUTURE VICTORY (Hebrews 11:22).

When you walk into Holy Trinity Church, Stratford-on-Avon, and walk down to the altar to the grave of William Shakespeare, you read the epitaph that he composed:

Good friend, for Jesus' sake forbear
To dig the dust enclosed here.
Blest be the man who spares these stones,
And curst be he who moves my bones.

Not very good poetry from a genius like Shakespeare, but he made his point: he didn't want his grave molested.

But both Joseph and his father had a different attitude toward their burial: they wanted to be moved! Jacob made Joseph promise that his body would not be buried in Egypt, but would be taken to the family burial cave at the Field of Machpelah. That's exactly what Joseph did (Genesis 47:29-31; 50:1-13). And when the time came for Joseph to die, he made his family promise that they would bury his body in the land of their inheritance.

Joseph did not want to be left in Egypt, even when he was dead! Joseph knew where he belonged. He was not an Egyptian; he was a Jew, and he belonged with his brethren in the land of their inheritance. He was a pilgrim to the very end, and he wanted the burial of a pilgrim.

After all, his burial would be his last opportunity to bear witness of his faith.

Joseph believed God's promise that the Jews would one day be led out of Egypt and brought to their own homeland. His father voiced that same promise (Genesis 48:4). In fact, the blessings that Jacob bestowed upon his sons and grandsons are absolutely meaningless apart from the Exodus. Jacob received the promise from Isaac, and Isaac certainly learned it from Abraham (Genesis 15:12-16).

Joseph died and was embalmed after the fashion of Egypt, and no doubt his body was placed in a prominent tomb. That tomb and that body were a constant reminder to the Jews that one day they would be set free from Egypt. Of course, at the time they did not realize the importance of that promise, because things were going well for them in Egypt. But when the new Pharaoh came to power, and the bitter bondage began, they found encouragement in the promise represented by Joseph's tomb.

Joseph not only knew where he belonged—in Canaan—but he knew what he believed! Joseph died, but the promise did not die.

It is really remarkable that Joseph had any faith at all. He certainly didn't get much encouragement at home. His brothers envied him, hated him, and finally sold him. It would have been easy for Joseph to say (as some people say today), "Well, if that's the way religious people behave, I want nothing to do with them or their faith!"

Not only was his family against his having strong faith, but circumstances seemed against him. Nothing seemed to go right for Joseph, even though he did his best to obey God and do what was right. His life seemed doomed from the start! Potiphar's wife lied about him, and this put him in prison. Then the butler forgot him, and that kept Joseph in prison. The people he helped didn't help him, and the promise he believed seemed to be impossible of fulfillment. Even God seemed to forget this courageous young man! "They afflicted his feet with fetters, he himself was laid in irons; until the time that his word came to pass, the word of the Lord tested him" (Psalm 105:18, 19).

Joseph was seventeen years old when he went to Egypt and thirty years old when he became the second ruler in the land; so he spent thirteen years under pagan Egyptian influence. Yet he remained a man of faith! The disappointments and delays didn't make him bitter. The memories of mistreatment by his brothers didn't rob him of his faith in God. Joseph certainly had many *excuses* he could have used for turning from the faith, but he had no *reasons*. He knew what he believed, and it was that faith that carried him through.

One night Joseph's tomb was emptied. It was the night of the Exodus when God delivered His people triumphantly from Egypt. "And Moses took the bones of Joseph with him, for he had made the sons of Israel solemnly swear, saying, 'God shall surely take care of you; and you shall carry my bones from here with you' " (Exodus 13:19). The very fact that the nation had Joseph's bones with them was an added encouragement to their faith. And when Israel had claimed their inheritance in the Promised Land, they buried Joseph's remains at Shechem (Joshua 24:32). God had kept His promise to the nation and the nation kept its promise to Joseph.

God is concerned about the human body. One day, each believer will have a new body, a body like Christ's glorious body. Why? Because, like Joseph, we know what we believe and where we belong. "For our citizenship is in heaven, from which also we eagerly wait for a Savior, the Lord Jesus Christ; who will transform the body of our humble state into conformity with the body of His glory . . ." (Philippians 3:20, 21). One day we shall participate in a glorious "Exodus" and enter fully into our inheritance!

All because of faith, faith for the future.

"Now faith is the assurance of things hoped for, the conviction of things not seen" (Hebrews 11:1).

By faith, the future is secure.

8/ WHEN FAITH SAYS "NO!"
HEBREWS 11:23-29

When faith says yes to God, it must also automatically say no to something else; otherwise the person is compromising. God demands total commitment to Him; we cannot serve two masters. Because Abraham believed God, he left Ur of the Chaldees and went to Canaan. He did not ask for a contract, nor did he try to negotiate terms with God. He simply obeyed. He said yes to God and no to Ur of the Chaldees. It took both decisions to make him a real man of faith.

It is relatively easy to say yes to God, but difficult to say no to the world, the flesh, and the devil. Lot said yes to God but never said no to the world, and the story of his pilgrimage ends in a cave where there is darkness, drunkenness, and debauchery. "Demas, having loved this present world, has deserted me," wrote Paul at a time when he desperately needed companionship and help (2 Timothy 4:10). In his classic allegory of the Christian life, *Pilgrim's Progress,* John Bunyan shows how many people joined Christian on his pilgrimage to the heavenly city, but then fell by the wayside because they would not say no to lesser things.

This paragraph describes the kind of faith that says no and sticks by the decision. The writer introduces Moses' parents, and then Moses himself, as well as the nation of Israel, and shows how their faith conquered Egypt.

1. FAITH TO DISOBEY THE LAWS OF EGYPT (Hebrews 11:23).

The names of Moses' parents were Amram and Jochebed (Exodus 6:20). They were obscure people, to be sure, but they gave to the world one of the greatest religious and political leaders in history. The background of the story is found in Exodus 2:1-10.

Jochebed had already given birth to two children, Miriam and Aaron, when Pharaoh issued his decree that all the male babies were to be drowned. Pharaoh was the first of many world rulers who was certain he could destroy the Jewish people; but, like all of his successors, he failed in his plans and almost destroyed himself.

When Moses was born, his mother knew that there was something special about her son. Since true faith is based on some word of revelation from God (Romans 10:17), we have to conclude that God gave Amram and Jochebed this divine indication that He had great plans for their son. Knowing that this murderous edict was being enforced, it certainly took faith for this husband and wife to engage in their normal marital life. They were both people of faith. They knew that conception and birth were in the hands of God.

How important it is for Christian parents to have cooperative faith! It is not enough for them to belong together; they must also believe together. The birth of Moses was not an accident; it was an appointment. The child was "lovely in the sight of God" (Acts 7:20) and therefore the parents knew that God would take care of him. How they must have prayed! How they must have reminded each other of the promises God had given

Abraham (Genesis 15:12-21). No doubt they rehearsed Joseph's prophecy that God would deliver the nation from the bondage of Egypt (Genesis 50:24, 25). This was God's Word, and faith grows when it is nurtured on the Word.

"You husbands likewise, live with your wives in an understanding way . . ." wrote the Apostle Peter, "and grant her honor as a fellow-heir of the grace of life, so that your prayers may not be hindered" (1 Peter 3:7). It was a time of trouble and tension for Israel, yet Amram and Jochebed loved each other, prayed together, and trusted God.

Their faith was not only cooperative, but it was also courageous. It took courage to disobey the law of Pharaoh. It also took courage to hide the child for three months and then put him into a little boat in the Nile River! What a paradox: Moses' life was saved by water, and Pharaoh's army was destroyed by water. Indeed, God "catches the wise in their craftiness" (1 Corinthians 3:19). Not only did Pharaoh's daughter rescue the child, but Pharaoh paid the wages for Moses' own mother to nurture the child.

There are times when faith in God demands that we disobey the edicts of men. Under ordinary circumstances, the Christian must obey the law and show respect to the governing authorities (Romans 13; Titus 3:1, 2; 1 Peter 2:13-17). But when the law of man is contrary to the Word of God, then the believer must, by faith, obey God. "We must obey God rather than men" (Acts 5:29).

This does not mean that the believer can oppose any law that he happens to dislike or that creates problems for him. He must be sure he has a definite word of faith from God. The Ten Commandments had not yet been given, yet Amram and Jochebed knew that it was wrong for them to slay the child God had given them.

When we do oppose the law, we must do it in a manner that glorifies God. A Christian has no right to create unnecessary problems for others, especially for unbelievers who have no understanding of spiritual matters.

Amram and Jochebed also had contagious faith: their daughter Miriam "caught it." Faith cannot be inherited, but it can be instilled; and Miriam realized that her parents *knew* that the baby boy would be preserved and protected. That explains Miriam's presence at the river, waiting to see what God would do. It also explains her swift action in securing a Hebrew nurse—her own mother—for the baby. She knew that God would prosper her efforts. God used a baby's tears and a sister's tact to rescue the future deliverer from the murderous hand of Pharaoh.

It is no wonder that Moses was a man of great faith, seeing he was nurtured by parents who had such courageous faith in God. Never underestimate the influence of a godly home. It can affect the destiny of a nation.

2. FAITH TO DEFY THE LIFE OF EGYPT
(Hebrews 11:24-26).

Many visitors to Rome find their way to the tomb of Pope Julius II, not necessarily because of the tomb or its occupant, but because there is a statue there that simply must be seen. It is Michelangelo's statue of Moses, one of the greatest pieces of sculpture that the master ever produced. A friend of mine keeps a small replica of this statue on his desk. He tells me that it encourages him whenever he looks at it and recalls all that God did in and through Moses.

Moses, of course, is much greater than any statue that even the most gifted sculptor could make of him. Whether you think of Moses the liberator, or Moses the law-giver, or Moses the spiritual leader, you are confronted with a man whose greatness increases the more you know about him. Moses is named ten times in the book of Hebrews, and the writer gives him this commen-

dation: "Now Moses was faithful in all His house as a
servant . . ." (3:5).

The key word in Moses' life is *refused*. Moses had the
faith to say no!

(a) *He refused position in Egypt* (Hebrews 11:24). "And
Moses was educated in all the learning of the Egyptians,"
Stephen said, "and he was a man of power in words and
deeds" (Acts 7:22). The fact that Moses was the adopted
son of the princess certainly gave him added advantages
over his peers; but Moses had natural abilities of his own.
Moses certainly didn't believe all that his Egyptian
teachers told him, but he listened just the same. Appar-
ently he held some government post and exercised his
authority with great skill and power.

Had Moses remained in the life of Egypt, no doubt he
could have attained great heights and achieved wonderful
things; *but he would not have been Moses!* God's plan
was not that he become Moses the Egyptian statesman,
or Moses the Egyptian scholar, but Moses the man of God.

This is not to say that everybody is supposed to do
what Moses did. God kept Joseph in the palace, and
Joseph was just as much a man of faith as Moses. Queen
Esther served God in the palace, and so did godly Daniel.
It is dangerous to make a blanket rule that forces everybody to do as Moses did, because God has different plans
for different lives. The important thing is that we act by
faith. It takes just as much faith to stay in the palace as to
leave it!

Certainly there were pressures to keep Moses in the
palace. For one thing, Pharaoh's daughter had saved his
life, and he owed something to her and her father. Some
of his associates might have argued that he could best
serve the enslaved Jews by remaining in government and
representing their cause. Moses had been separated from
his nation for so long that in many ways he was more an
Egyptian than a Hebrew. In fact, Jethro's daughters

thought Moses *was* an Egyptian (Exodus 2:19).

But faith doesn't weigh alternatives; it acts on assurances. Moses knew that God wanted him out of the palace and identified with the people of Israel. To those around him, his decision seemed foolish, even dangerous; but to Moses, his decision was in the will of God. With one decision of faith, the ruler became a servant. Tho man who was the pride of the court identified himself with the Jewish slaves! It was a decision not unlike that one recorded in Philippians 2.

(b) *He refused pleasures in Egypt* (Hebrews 11:25). When Moses made his great decision, he knew that he was entering into a life of suffering and sorrow. Life would have been much easier for him had he remained a leader in Egypt, except for one thing: to remain in the palace would have been sinful. We must not interpret "the passing pleasures of sin" to mean the gross sensual activities of a place such as Corinth. To be sure, there was plenty of sin in Egypt, and a man of influence such as Moses could have had his share. For Moses, "the passing pleasures of sin" would mean the ease and affluence of the palace as compared with the trials and sufferings of his people. Whatever he did as an Egyptian officer would never last, but whatever he did in the service of God would last forever.

Each of us must decide: am I going to *enjoy* my life in my own way, or am I going to *employ* my life in the will of God. This is not to suggest that there is no enjoyment in serving God, because there certainly is. It is simply a question of living for the immediate or the eternal.

Paul the apostle made a similar decision. He was one of the leading rabbis of his day, "advancing in Judaism beyond many of my contemporaries among my countrymen, being more extremely zealous for my ancestral traditions" (Galatians 1:14). He had a bright future ahead of him, but he refused all of it that he might serve Christ

(Philippians 3:7-10). To remain a religious teacher of the Jews would have been, for Paul, enjoying "the passing pleasures of sin."

At the beginning of the life of faith, you make decisions on the basis of "good" and "bad." But as you grow in faith, you make decisions on the basis of "better" and "best." Men and women of faith can't waste their lives on that which is passing; they build on that which is permanent. This explains why they are often misunderstood, even called crazy. They simply are not interested in the plans and pleasures of the unbelieving world. They have seen the glory of God and, in comparison, everything the world has to offer is but rubbish.

(c) *He refused promises from Egypt* (Hebrews 11:26). Life is built on character, and character is built on decisions. Moses was a man of character because he made the right decisions. Man is both the sculptor and the marble, and the decisions he makes help to determine his character. Somebody asked the great financier J. P. Morgan what was the best collateral a man could give, and the banker replied, "Character!" Moses was not concerned about his reputation when he made his decision; he was concerned about character.

Life is built on character, and character is built on decisions. But decisions are built on *values*. We make our choices on the basis of the things that are important to us.

An unbelieving Egyptian, looking at Moses, would conclude that this prince had everything worth living for: prestige, authority, wealth, a challenging future. But believing Moses looked at those same things and decided they were cheap! He wanted neither the pleasures nor the treasures of Egypt because he had something far better: the reproach of Christ and the reward of God.

The key verb here is "considering" (v. 26). The word means "to reckon, to evaluate." Moses made the right decision because he had the right values. The people of God were of more value to him than the pleasures and treasures of Egypt. Reproach for Christ was better than fame in Egypt. The eternal was more important than the temporal, even though it meant hardship and suffering.

How could Moses identify with "the reproach of Christ" when Christ had not yet come? When you remember the persons to whom the book of Hebrews was sent, you answer the question. They were Jewish believers who were suffering for their faith, and who were tempted to return to the ease and comfort of Judaism. They were facing the same decision that Moses faced. Jesus Christ bore reproach for us; should we not bear reproach for Him? "Hence, let us go out to Him outside the camp, bearing His reproach" (Hebrews 13:13).

What enabled Moses to do this? "He was looking to the reward" (11:26). Men and women of faith are always people with vision. They see what others do not see, and this vision helps to determine their values. The verb in verse 26 implies continuous action: "he kept looking away with fixed attention on the reward." Moses was not distracted by the pleasures of Egypt—even the good things—but kept his attention fixed on the things of God.

Nothing weakens the life of faith like distractions. The secret of victory is "fixing our eyes on Jesus, the author and perfecter of faith" (Hebrews 12:2). Moses' decisions were based on values, and those values were based on faith. Because he believed God, he knew what was really important in life. He was not impressed by the grandeur of Egypt, for his eyes had caught the vision of the city of God. Like the patriarchs, "he was looking for the city which has foundations, whose architect and builder is God" (11:10).

Life is built on character, character is built on decisions, decisions are built on values, and values are built on faith. But this faith comes from the Word of God (Romans 10:17), so, ultimately, our values must come from God's Word. As you read the Bible, especially the life of our Lord, you discover that what is important to the world is not always important to God. The world is too often concerned about prices, not values, and the price tags are all confused. Men measure wealth in terms of how much they own, yet Jesus said that a man's life does not consist of the abundance of what he possesses (Luke 12:15). And Paul's warning is "the things which are seen are temporal, but the things which are not seen are eternal" (2 Corinthians 4:18).

Moses knew that God rewards faith. He may not give the reward immediately, or even in this life; but the promised reward is sure to come. The Egyptians reminded Moses of what he was losing, but God reminded him of what he was gaining; and his gains were far greater than his losses.

In every way, Moses' decision of faith utterly defied the life of Egypt. He refused position in Egypt, the pleasures of Egypt, and the promises of Egypt, that he might do the will of God. He never regretted his decision. Though the people of Israel often wanted to go back to Egypt, not once did Moses court that desire. By faith Moses buried Egypt! His eyes had, by faith, caught a vision far greater than anything Egypt had to offer, and he was determined to press on to that great goal. When your values are based on faith, they don't fluctuate with the changing standards of the world.

Moses was a man of godly character because he was a man of right decisions; for character is built on decisions. But his decisions were based on godly values, and those values were based on faith. This is what made Moses such a great man; and, while you and I may never be called upon to do the deeds of Moses, we can still share the same kind of character because our decisions and values are from God. The world is concerned about popularity and reputation, but the people who walk by faith are concerned about character and the glory of God.

3. FAITH TO DEPART FROM THE LAND OF EGYPT
(Hebrews 11:27-29).

The focus now is on the nation, with Moses as the leader;
but the emphasis is still on faith. The vision of faith led
to these victories of faith. It is always the man and woman
of faith who can lead others out of their bondage and into
the blessings God has prepared for them. Faith in God
gave Moses the courage to defy the powers of Egypt and
deliver the people of God from slavery. Moses was not
afraid of the king's anger (v. 27), the king's authority
(v. 28), or the king's army (v. 29).

(a) *The king's anger* (11:27). What event is this verse
describing? Some believe it is referring to Moses' sudden
escape from Egypt after it was discovered that he had
killed a man (Exodus 2:11-22); but this interpretation
presents some problems. For one thing, Exodus 2:14
clearly states that Moses *was* afraid. Pharaoh was out to
kill Moses, so Moses fled from Egypt and spent the next
forty years living in Midian. Furthermore, the Greek verb
translated "he left" means "to leave behind once and for
all." When Moses fled to Midian, it was only a temporary
thing; he did return to Egypt. When Moses left for Midian, it was a hasty retreat; but Hebrews 11:27 suggests a
deliberate and studied decision. It would appear that
Hebrews 11:27 is talking about that final exodus from
Egypt when Moses led his people to freedom.

But what about the anger of the king? When you consider Pharaoh's attitude during his last meeting with
Moses and Aaron, you have no problem with this statement. "Get away from me!" Pharaoh said to Moses and
Aaron. "Beware, do not see my face again, for in the day
you see my face you shall die!" (Exodus 10:28). He was an
angry man, at the end of his rope! Even though on Passover night, Pharaoh begged Moses to leave (Exodus 12:31,
32), his heart changed after that and he was determined
to avenge himself on Israel (Exodus 14:5ff.).

Keep in mind that Pharaoh was like a god to the people of Egypt. He had absolute power over the nation and he answered to nobody for what he did. He had only to give the order and a citizen would be killed. All the while Moses was ministering in Egypt, his life was in jeopardy. He never knew when Pharaoh would have a fit of anger and order Moses to be slain. This danger increased as the plagues progressed, and it reached its climax on Passover night. Moses was a marked man, and he knew it; yet he was not afraid.

The secret? "He endured, as seeing Him who is unseen" (Hebrews 11:27). Like the patriarchs of old (11:10, 13-16), Moses had eyes of faith. He looked beyond Pharaoh and Egypt and saw God! Once you have caught the vision of the greatness and glory of God, you will not be afraid of kings or armies. "The Lord is my helper, I will not be afraid. What shall man do to me?" (Hebrews 13:6).

It has well been said that the greatest ability is dependability. Without dependability, all other abilities are useless. The people to whom Hebrews was written were tempted to quit. Life was just too much for them and it was costing them to maintain their Christian testimony. "Be like Moses!" the writer is saying. "He endured because he kept his eyes of faith fixed on the Lord!" These Hebrew Christians were afraid of the anger of their unbelieving relatives and friends; in fact, they had already suffered persecution and even the spoiling of their goods (10:32-39). "Don't be afraid!" is the message of this section. "Faith will see you through!"

(b) *The king's authority* (Hebrews 11:28). Pharaoh would not permit the Jews to leave Egypt to worship God (Exodus 5:1ff.). In spite of repeated judgments on the land, and untold suffering to his people, Pharaoh hardened his heart and refused to submit to the authority of Jehovah God. But the Lord had one plague more—the visitation of the angel of death. Only those found in houses marked by the blood would be delivered from death.

It certainly required faith for Moses and his people to obey the instructions for Passover. The only assurance they had that their firstborn would not die was the promise of the Word of God. They could not go by past history because there had never been such an event as this before. They certainly could not go by their personal feelings. No doubt many of them sat in their houses trembling, and yet they were still safe and secure. Because they believed the Word of God, they were protected from the angel of death.

And yet the whole procedure at Passover seemed so foolish! How could the blood of a lamb protect a household from death? Why must the blood be applied to the door by a flimsy little bush called hyssop? What guarantee was there that all of this would work? *The promise of the word of God.* You had to make a choice that night: either believe the authority of Pharaoh's word or the authority of God's word. The Egyptians had faith, but their faith was misdirected: they trusted the word of Pharaoh, and their firstborn died. The difference between a saved person and an unsaved person is not that one has faith while the other does not. The difference is in the *object* of faith: the unbeliever trusts the word of man, but the believer trusts the Word of God. Faith is only as good as the object.

The issue is clear: faith means life, unbelief means death. If we trust God's Word and act upon it, we have nothing to fear.

(c) *The king's army* (Hebrews 11:29). Faith not only brings us out, but it also takes us through. God completes what He starts; He is the "author and perfecter of faith" (Hebrews 12:2).

Redemption is but the beginning of the life of faith. It is

one thing to be set free and quite another thing to defeat the enemies that want to rob you of your freedom. Once Pharaoh got over the shock of the death of the firstborn, he realized that he was losing valuable slave labor in the departure of Israel; so he sent his armies to stop the Jews and return them to Egypt. The dramatic story is told in Exodus 14.

From the human point of view, Israel was in an impossible situation. The Red Sea stood before them, the wilderness around them, and the Egyptian army behind them! *God is glorified in impossible situations.* When human resources are gone, then divine resources can go to work on behalf of those who trust God.

It is interesting to see how different people respond when the going is tough. Many of the Jews became frightened (Exodus 14:10), while others in their fear started to blame Moses (14:11). "Leave us alone that we may serve the Egyptians," they cried (v. 12). No sooner were they delivered from Egypt than they wanted to go back! (Again, here is the theme of Hebrews: "Let us go on. . . .") The night was gathering around them, and everything seemed to be lost.

But Moses interceded on behalf of Israel, and God rescued them. (Again, another theme of Hebrews is the intercessory work of Christ, the great High Priest.) He sent a strong east wind all that night. No doubt most of the Jews thought that wind was working against them, when it was in reality working for them. The next day, when Moses stretched out his rod, God opened the sea and took the nation through safely. When the Egyptians tried to follow, they were all drowned!

You have never really trusted God until you have trusted Him for the impossible. Saving faith in Christ brings us out, but it is sustaining faith that brings us through. "He who did not spare His own Son, but delivered Him up for us all, how will He not also with Him freely give us all things?" (Romans 8:32).

It took but one night for God to take Israel out of Egypt, but it took forty years to take Egypt out of Israel. Whenever the going got tough, some of the people immediately began to talk about retreating back to Egypt. They failed to understand that the God who saved them was able to keep them and fulfill in them all His perfect will. When we walk by sight, we see only the difficulties; but when we walk by faith, we see the possibilities. The same situation that drowns an unbeliever only delivers the believer, because his trust is in God alone.

Believers today must make a choice between the world (Egypt) and the will of God; faith in man or faith in God.

Jesus Christ "gave Himself for our sins, that He might deliver us out of this present evil age" (Galatians 1:4).

He has brought us out, and He is able to bring us through.

The question is not His ability, but our faith.

Do you have faith to say no to this world and yes to God?

9/ JOSHUA AND RAHAB: FAITH IS THE VICTORY
HEBREWS 11:30, 31; JOSHUA 1—6

It would be difficult to find two more opposite people than Joshua and Rahab. One was a Jewish general, the other a Gentile prostitute. Joshua was a member of the covenant nation, while Rahab was a foreigner, an outcast. Joshua was the conqueror while Rahab was among the conquered. What, then, brings them together? *Their faith.* Both Joshua and Rahab won the victory over Jericho because they believed God. Joshua won a military victory and Rahab won a spiritual victory. In both cases, the secret was faith.

1. JOSHUA—VICTORY OVER THE ENEMY (Hebrews 11:30).

Between verses 29 and 30 are forty years of Israel's wandering in the wilderness; yet not one word is said about it. Why? Because those were years of unbelief, and Hebrews 11 celebrates faith. In chapters 3 through 5, the writer of Hebrews uses Israel's failure as a warning against unbelief, so he does not ignore the facts of history. But in this chapter, the focus is on faith and its victories, not on unbelief and its defeats.

Three important lessons are found in Joshua's experience.

(a) *God brings us out that He might bring us in.* The geography of the Bible is important and illustrates basic spiritual truth. Egypt, of course, typifies the world system. The unsaved person, like the children of Israel, is in bondage to this present evil world and cannot deliver himself (Ephesians 2:1-3).

Canaan is a picture of the believer's inheritance in Jesus Christ. Canaan is *not* a picture of heaven, no matter what the song writers might say. Israel experienced both fights and failures in Canaan, something that surely cannot happen in heaven. Under the leadership of Joshua, the Jews claimed their inheritance by faith and defeated the enemy.

The wilderness between Egypt and Canaan pictures the life of unbelief that Christians experience when they fail to surrender to God and believe Him for victory. The Jews were delivered from Egypt by the blood of the lamb and the power of God, just as Christians today are redeemed by our Lord's death and resurrection. We have a rich inheritance in Christ "in the heavenly places" (Ephesians 1:3) if only we will claim it by faith. It is a life of battles and blessings, challenges and growth, and even occasional defeats and discouragements. But always, it is a life of faith.

Alas, not many of God's people enter into this life of faith and victory. They still have an appetite for Egypt instead of a vision for Canaan. Instead of heeding the call, "let us press on to maturity" (Hebrews 6:1), they yearn to go back into slavery. They are unwilling to pay the price that victorious faith demands. Instead of believing warriors, they are unbelieving wanderers, wasting their lives and opportunities in the wilderness when they could be enjoying their inheritance.

Moses said it perfectly: "And He brought us out from

there [Egypt] in order to bring us in . . ." (Deuteronomy 6:23). Whatever God starts, He finishes. He is "the author and perfecter of faith" (Hebrews 12:2). Had Israel believed God at Kadesh-barnea, they would have entered the land, claimed their inheritance, and saved themselves forty years of the world's longest funeral march, as a whole generation died in unbelief.

How was Israel redeemed from Egypt? *By faith.*

How did Israel cross the Red Sea? *By faith.*

How was Israel to enter Canaan and claim the inheritance? *By faith.*

As Christians, we were saved by faith and we must live by faith. The same God who started this marvelous life in us is able to develop it and perfect it so that we can enjoy all that He has planned for us.

Note that it was Joshua, not Moses, who led the people into their inheritance. Moses represents the law, and we cannot claim our spiritual inheritance by keeping the law. The name Joshua means "Jehovah is salvation" and is the Old Testament equivalent of the name Jesus. We claim our spiritual inheritance by yielding ourselves by faith to Jesus, the Son of God. Through His death, burial, resurrection, and ascension, He has defeated every foe and opened up the way for us to enter into the promised inheritance.

When Israel crossed the Red Sea, it meant death to the old life of slavery in Egypt. When Israel crossed the Jordan River and entered into Canaan, it meant death to the wasted life of unbelief in the wilderness. Yes, it took faith to walk across that riverbed; but that was the only way they could claim their inheritance. It took faith to confront walled cities and strong armies, but it was faith that gave them the victory "For whatever is born of God overcomes the world; and this is the victory that has overcome the world—our faith" (1 John 5:4).

It is not enough to say, "I am saved!" Can you also say, "I am enjoying my inheritance in Christ"?

(b) *God brings us in that we might overcome.* In the wilderness, Israel *was* overcome; but in Canaan, Israel *did* overcome. The life of faith is, as we have already noted, a life of battles as well as blessings. Once we enter into the promised land, the enemy attacks us and tries to discourage us and defeat us. This explains why the Lord said to Joshua, "Be strong and courageous, for you shall give this people possession of the land which I swore to their fathers to give them. Only be strong and very courageous . . ." (Joshua 1:6, 7).

Where can we get the strength and courage that we need to face the enemy and claim the victory? We can get these blessings only as we trust God's Word. It is here that Israel's conquest of Jericho becomes an object lesson of the victory that comes through faith. You and I overcome the enemy and claim the inheritance in the same way that Joshua conquered Jericho.

The city of Jericho was impregnable. There was no human means available to defeat it. But Joshua knew that, since God had brought him and the people to that place, He had a plan for taking the city. People who walk by faith don't see obstacles; they see opportunities. Forty years before, the spies had seen only the obstacles: ". . . the people who live in the land are strong, and the cities are fortified and very large; and moreover, we saw the descendants of Anak there" (Numbers 13:28). Their conclusion? "We are not able to go up against the people, for they are too strong for us!" (Numbers 13:31).

They forgot that God brought them out so that He might bring them in, and that He brings His people in so that they might overcome the enemy and claim the inheritance. They were walking by sight and not by faith. They were listening to their fears instead of to God's promises. As a result, they discouraged the people; and God had to wait for forty years for that whole generation of "unbelieving believers" to die. The only sentence God can pass on unbelief is death.

Just before the battle, Joshua went out to survey the

situation, and suddenly he met a stranger. Here is the record:

> Now it came about when Joshua was by Jericho, that he lifted up his eyes and looked, and behold, a man was standing opposite him with his sword drawn in his hand, and Joshua went to him and said to him, "Are you for us or for our adversarsies?" And he said, "No, rather I indeed come now as captain of the host of the Lord." And Joshua fell on his face to the earth, and bowed down, and said to him, "What has my lord to say to his servant?" And the captain of the Lord's host said to Joshua, "Remove your sandals from your feet, for the place where you are standing is holy." And Joshua did so. Joshua 5:13-15

It was Jesus Christ that Joshua met, and that meeting was the assurance of victory. Public victories are the outcome of private meetings with the Lord. When Joshua faced Jericho, he knew he was not alone: the Lord was with him. Furthermore, he discovered that he was second in command! All he had to do was take orders from the Lord and the victory was secure. "See," said the Lord, "I have given Jericho into your hand . . ." (Joshua 6:2). He had already won the victory! All Joshua had to do was follow orders and, by faith, claim the city for God.

Because the city was already defeated, it really made little difference what means God wanted to use to bring about the victory. In the case of Jericho, the approach seemed foolish; but it was still God's plan. They were to march around the city in silence once a day for six days. Then they were to march around the city seven times on the seventh day. (By this time, the spectators on the wall must have been terribly curious!) At the end of the seventh march, the people were to shout, and the priests were to blow their trumpets; and the wall would fall down flat.

And that's exactly the way it happened!

Faith is not in a hurry, and faith is not worried when people say, "That's foolish!" God still chooses the foolish things of this world to shame the wise and the weak things to shame the strong (1 Corinthians 1:26-29). He uses Moses' rod, and the priests' trumpets, and David's sling, and a little boy's lunch. He even used a Roman cross! God's methods and tools may seem foolish, but faith in God is not foolish. While the wise men of the world are shaking their heads in disbelief, the children of God are lifting their hearts in joyful faith and watching God do miracles.

The victory of Jericho was not the result of "great faith" so much as faith in a great God. The generation of Jews buried in the wilderness were *overcome,* but the generation in Canaan were *overcomers.* The difference? Faith in God's Word.

The next time, in the will of God, you face a Jericho situation in your life, pause to find out what God's battle plan is, and dare to believe it and obey it. What He asks you to do may seem foolish, but that is where faith comes in. It bears repeating: faith is not believing in spite of evidence; it is obeying in spite of circumstance or consequence.

"In the world you have tribulation," our Lord said to His disciples, "but take courage; I have overcome the world" (John 16:33). The world system around us builds high its Jerichos, and dares us to attack them; but the believer knows that every stronghold of the enemy *has already been defeated at the Cross.* We do not fight *for* victory; we fight *from* victory. And the weapons we use are not the weapons of men. "For the weapons of our warfare are not of the flesh, but divinely powerful for the destruction of fortresses" (2 Corinthians 10:4). Paul may have had Jericho in mind when he wrote those words.

Not only has Christ conquered the world and its fortresses, but He has also defeated the flesh and the devil. "Now those who belong to Christ Jesus have crucified the flesh with its passions and desires" (Galatians 5:24). "Now judgment is upon this world; now the ruler of this world shall be cast out" (John 12:31). Even our last enemy—death—has been defeated at the Cross! "O death, where is your victory? O death, where is your sting?" (1 Corinthians 15:55).

God brings us out that He might bring us in, and He brings us in that we might overcome. There is a third lesson we learn from Joshua's faith:

(c) *We overcome so that we might claim our inheritance.* The emphasis in Hebrews is on the believer and his inheritance. At the very opening of the book, the writer presents Jesus Christ as the Son of God "whom He appointed heir of all things" (1:2). The believers are called "those who will inherit salvation" (1:14) and "the heirs of the promise" (6:17). Through Jesus Christ we have "the promise of the eternal inheritance" (9:15). Both Noah and Abraham are associated with an inheritance (11:7, 8).

How rich we are in Jesus Christ! The Father has "blessed us with every spiritual blessing in the heavenly places in Christ" (Ephesians 1:3). God's "divine power has granted to us everything pertaining to life and godliness" (2 Peter 1:3). Every spiritual blessing! Everything! The inheritance is there for us to claim by faith.

What keeps us from claiming what is rightfully ours in Christ? Sometimes it is our spiritual lethargy that is to blame: "that you may not be sluggish, but imitators of those who through faith and patience inherit the promises" (Hebrews 6:12). When circumstances are difficult, we get impatient and run ahead of God, instead of waiting by faith for Him to work things out.

But our greatest obstacle is unbelief. Like the Jews at Kadesh-barnea (Numbers 13, 14), we simply will not believe God's Word and so we try to go back to Egypt! When the race of faith gets too hard for us, we start to buckle in the knees and give up.

It is interesting to compare Joshua 1:3 and Ephesians 1:3.

Every place on which the sole of your foot treads, I have given it to you, just as I spoke to Moses.	*Blessed be the God and Father of our Lord Jesus Christ, who has blessed us with every spiritual blessing in the heavenly places in Christ.*

Joshua was not stealing anything from anybody, for everything in Canaan had already been given to him and his people. All they had to do was to step out by faith and claim it. When we read the book of Joshua, we discover that Israel's only defeats were caused by unbelief, disobedience, and running ahead of God. So long as they trusted God, they marched forward in victory.

Our inheritance is in the heavenlies, and Satan is opposing the church in the heavenlies (Ephesians 6:10ff.). This means that we cannot claim our inheritance without a battle. We must keep in mind that our battles are not with flesh and blood—the people who cause problems in our lives—but with the satanic forces that control these people. Satan is already a defeated foe, so we can oppose him without fear. We should remember that, like Joshua, we are second in command. If we trust the Lord of hosts, He will lead us to victory.

2. RAHAB—VICTORY OVER SIN (Hebrews 11:31).
Sarah and Rahab are the only women who are actually named in this chapter, although Moses' mother is inferred in verse 23, Pharaoh's daughter is mentioned in verse 24, and in verse 35 we meet "women [who] received back their dead. . . ." The Church ought to sing "Faith of Our Mothers" as well as "Faith of Our Fathers."

So important is Rahab in Bible history that she is

mentioned three times in the New Testament, in Matthew
1:5; Hebrews 11:31; and James 2:25. How remarkable that
a heathen prostitute should be named in the genealogy of
Jesus Christ. What a testimony of the grace of God!

The emphasis in Hebrews 11:31 is on *saving faith.*
Because Rahab had saving faith, she and her family did
not perish when Jericho was taken by the Israelites. We
find the account in Joshua 2; 6:20-25. When we examine
the life of Rahab, we discover four vital lessons about
saving faith.

(a) *The importance of saving faith.* It is found in one
word: *condemnation.* Rahab was a condemned woman
living in a condemned city. God's commission to Israel
was that they defeat the enemy and utterly destroy them
(Deuteronomy 7:1-6, 23-26; 12:1-3). It was not a question
of whether the inhabitants of Jericho *felt* condemned;
they *were* condemned, according to the Word of God. The
citizens may have trusted their great city walls, but they
were still under the condemnation of God. Life may have
gone on as usual all the while Israel was camped by
Jericho, but the city was marked for judgment just the
same.

Was God being unmerciful to the citizens of Jericho?
No, not in the least. He should have wiped out these
godless people back in Abraham's day, but He postponed
His judgment for over four hundred years (Genesis 15:14-
21). He waited another forty years after the Exodus,
knowing that the news of this great event would carry to
Jericho (Joshua 2:10). After Israel arrived at the Jordan,
they waited another week; and then they marched around
the city for a week. Talk about the patience of God!

We must keep in mind that Canaan was populated by
nations that were morally evil. We have only to read the
warnings in Deuteronomy to realize how wicked they
were, not only in their daily lives, but in their religious
practices. When Joshua wiped out these nations, he was

cleaning out a sewer, so filthy was their conduct. At one time, these people had known the true God; but they preferred not to trust Him or obey Him (Romans 1:18ff.). They were sinning against a flood of light, and not a single citizen could ever claim that he did not have a chance to repent and be saved.

Why is saving faith important? Because lost sinners are under condemnation and can be saved only through faith in Jesus Christ. "He who believes in Him is not judged; he who does not believe has been judged already, because he has not believed in the name of the only begotten Son of God. . . . He who believes in the Son has eternal life; but he who does not obey the Son shall not see life, but the wrath of God abides on him" (John 3:18, 36).

Rahab was a condemned woman. She was morally condemned as a prostitute, and racially condemned as a Gentile who was outside the covenant family of God. Furthermore, she *knew* she was condemned, for the terror of God had fallen upon all of the people (Joshua 2:9-11). The fact that God's judgment had been delayed all those long centuries did not give her a false confidence. After all, the long-suffering of God means salvation for those who will trust Him, but judgment for those who delay (2 Peter 3:8, 9). It is dangerous to presume upon the patience of God. "Because the sentence against an evil deed is not executed quickly, therefore the hearts of the sons of men among them are given fully to do evil" (Ecclesiastes 8:11).

(b) *The nature of saving faith.* Rahab was not saved from judgment because she had faith in herself, or because she had faith in faith. True saving faith is much more than superstitious "hope so" or mere intellectual assent. True saving faith involves the whole person.

To begin with, saving faith involves *the mind.* There were certain facts that Rahab knew and believed (Joshua 2:8-11). She knew that Jehovah was the true God, and that Israel were the people of God. She heard of the great works of Jehovah in delivering Israel from Egypt. She said, "For the Lord your God, He is God in heaven above and on earth beneath" (Joshua 2:11). Rahab knew that she was a condemned woman, along with all the other citizens of Jericho; and that her only hope was to fall on the mercy and grace of God.

Saving faith also involves *the emotions.* The fear of God was in her heart. "And when we heard it, our hearts melted and no courage remained in any man any longer . . ." (Joshua 2:11). One of the obstacles to saving faith is "There is no fear of God before their eyes" (Romans 3:18). "The fear of the Lord is the beginning of knowledge" (Proverbs 1:7).

Is fear a proper motive for salvation? Of course it is! The fear of injury, sickness, and death plays an important role in the decisions people make every single day. John the Baptist in his preaching warned sinners about the wrath to come, and even Jesus preached about the fires of hell (Matthew 3:7-12; 23:33; 25:30). Only the most hardhearted sinner could contemplate the awesomeness of the final judgment and remain unmoved.

But it takes more than an enlightened mind and a stirred heart for a sinner to be saved. Rahab's saving faith also involved *her will.* Because she believed the truth, she acted upon it. She treated the spies with kindness and made them promise that, when the city was taken, she and her family would be spared (Joshua 2:12-14). She openly confessed her faith in the God of Israel and asked for mercy!

In my ministry, I have met people who thought they had saving faith, but their faith was incomplete. Some had mere intellectual assent to the biblical facts of history. Others experienced an emotional stirring, but they never gave evidence of true repentance. Still others tried to please God with their obedience and good works. They stopped their bad habits and deserted their evil company.

But this kind of "faith" is not saving faith because it is

incomplete. It does not involve the whole person. Rahab knew the truth in her mind and felt the fear in her heart. By an act of her own will, she confessed the God of Israel and trusted Him to save her. *And she risked her life to do it!*

(c) *The evidences of saving faith.* In Rahab's case, we see at least three evidences that her faith was real.

First of all, *she had assurance in her heart.* "I know that the Lord has given you the land . . ." (Joshua 2:9). When we put our faith in God's Word, He gives us the witness of the Spirit in our hearts, and we have assurance.

Second, *her life was changed.* She proved her faith by her works (James 2:25, 26). Nobody is saved by works, or even by faith plus works. We are saved by a faith that results in works. The fact that she hid the spies and cooperated with them was proof that her faith was real.

Third, *she won others.* She immediately began to intercede for her lost loved ones. "Spare my father and my mother and my brothers and my sisters, with all who belong to them, and deliver our lives from death" (Joshua 2:13). She shared her witness with her family, and they, too, were saved. Religious people can promote their religion, but only saved people can share *life.* Living faith is contagious; we have to share it with others.

(d) *The rewards of saving faith.* The first reward was her own escape from terrible judgment. As soon as the city had been taken, Joshua commanded his soldiers to utterly destroy everything (Joshua 6:21). However, he ordered the men to bring out Rahab and her family and set them outside the camp in a place of safety. They stood there and watched Jericho burn!

No matter how the unbeliever may twist the Scriptures and try to argue, there is fire in his future. There is a "wrath to come" (1 Thessalonians 1:10; 5:9). One day, "the

Lord Jesus shall be revealed from heaven with His mighty angels in flaming fire, dealing out retribution to those who do not know God and to those who do not obey the gospel of our Lord Jesus" (2 Thessalonians 1:7, 8). Rahab and her family escaped the fire because they had saving faith.

This leads to a second reward of saving faith, *the joy of reaching others.* It has well been said that the gospel is good news, and good news is for sharing! No sooner did Matthew the publican trust Christ than he wanted to share Him with his sinner friends. When the woman at the well (John 4) tasted the living water, she left her water pot and went into the city to share her discovery with others.

A third reward is even more wonderful: *Rahab actually became a part of Israel!* According to Matthew 1:5, she married a Jewish man named Salmon, and actually became an ancestress of our Lord Jesus Christ (Ruth 4:18-22). Not only was she rescued from the fire, but she ended up at a wedding! This outcast Gentile pagan became a member of the covenant nation of Israel!

Rahab's faith certainly rebukes unbelievers today. She had only a meager amount of information, yet she believed and was saved. There was nobody in Jericho to encourage her, yet she held to her belief until the promised deliverance was fulfilled. Her faith was perhaps imperfect—she lied about the spies—but still she trusted God.

Today we have a whole Bible, not just a fragmented rumor; and the message we hear is one of love and salvation, not wrath and condemnation. "For God did not send the Son into the world to judge the world; but that the world should be saved through Him" (John 3:17). We are surrounded by people who have trusted Christ, people who encourage us to be saved. Rahab risked her life to believe, yet we today have every encouragement to trust Jesus Christ and be saved.

Rahab will rise in judgment against this generation!
Will she rise up in judgment against you?

The experience of Rahab makes it clear that nobody is
too bad to be saved, or too ignorant to be saved; but you
can be *too late* to be saved.

"Behold, now is 'the acceptable time,' behold, now is
'the day of salvation' " (2 Corinthians 6:2).

10/ *TIME IS RUNNING OUT*
HEBREWS 11:32–35a

It happens in almost every church: a name is omitted from the list and somebody's feelings are hurt. Perhaps the pastor was thanking those who worked in Vacation Bible School, and he failed to mention two bus drivers, or the lady who mixed the punch. Or perhaps the church secretary was listing in the bulletin the names of the people who helped to clean the church building, and omitted a couple of names.

What do you do? You apologize and include them next Sunday!

But the writer of Hebrews 11 knew that it was impossible to name everybody who had successfully run the race of faith and brought glory to the Lord. Not all the giants of faith are named in this chapter because of a lack of time and space. (John had the same problem when he was writing about the miracles that Jesus performed—John 21:25.) So the writer closes chapter 11 with a summary of some of the people God used and the things they accomplished by faith.

By the way, not only this summary, but the entire chapter reminds us of the importance of knowing the

Old Testament Scriptures. The Old Testament may not be the easiest book to read and understand, but it is certainly important to the life of the Christian. Remember, the only "Bible" that Jesus, the apostles, and the early church had was the Old Testament! Hebrews 11 makes it clear that the Old Testament is *a record of faith.* As we read about Moses, David, Daniel, and these other heroes, our own faith ought to grow.

The Old Testament is not only a record of faith, but also a record of discipline. The way God dealt with His people ought to instruct us and warn us not to play with sin (1 Corinthians 10:11). As we read the Old Testament, we ought to grow in our faith and hope (Romans 5:4), and certainly we ought to see the Lord Jesus Christ (Luke 24:27).

So, don't ignore or neglect the Old Testament. As the old adage puts it: "The New is in the Old concealed, and the Old is in the New revealed." The whole Word of God is inspired and profitable, so read and study in both the Old Testament and the New Testament.

What are the encouraging lessons found in this summary?

1. GOD USES A VARIETY OF PERSONS.

As we read this passage, we discover quite a mixture of different kinds of people. There are both men and women, young and old. There are "official people" (kings and prophets) and common people, such as you and me. Some of these were "high born," while others had no special pedigree. I see in this list farmers, shepherds, soldiers, priests, and even the son of a prostitute (Jephthah).

What brought these people together? *Faith.*

Just about everything about our first birth separates us from others. We all have a different heredity, different tastes and interests, different skills. The Declaration of

Independence may state that "all men are created equal," but that doesn't mean that everybody is alike. We are equal before God as sinners and equal before the law as citizens, but we are not equal to each other.

It is the second birth that brings us together! We share a common faith and a common life. Though our human differences still exist, they don't create problems because all of us are indwelt by the same Spirit and desire to glorify the same Lord. There is diversity in the midst of unity.

What did these people have in common? For one thing, they all heard God's Word and were stirred by what they heard. They believed it and acted upon it, and God used them to accomplish great things. They were not perfect by any means, but God used them to further His purposes and honor His name.

In verse 32, the writer mentions three periods in Israel's history: the Judges (Gideon, Barak, Samson, Jephthah), the Kings (David), and the Prophets (Samuel and the prophets). Faith is not limited to one period in history or even to one kind of political system. Before there was an official kingdom, the judges were doing great exploits by faith. When the kingdom degenerated, God raised up the prophets to demonstrate the power of faith. We must never say that faith cannot operate because of the "times" or the "circumstances," because true faith is not limited by history.

Faith, then, doesn't depend on IQ (although some intelligence is necessary to know God's Word), or physical or psychological equipment; nor does faith depend on the circumstances around us. Gideon with three hundred soldiers, or Samson by himself, can exercise faith and accomplish God's purposes. We must never say, "God can't do anything here!" God is not limited by circumstances, but He is limited by our unbelief. "And He could do no miracle there . . . and He wondered at their unbelief" (Mark 6:5, 6).

2. FAITH SOLVES A VARIETY OF PROBLEMS.
There are two ways to look at history: what men are
doing, and what God is doing through men. Dr. A. T.
Pierson used to say, "History is His story." The secular
historian, examining the history of Israel, would see
leaders, battles, victories, and great achievements—but
he would not see *faith*. Apart from faith in God, the
history of Israel is a puzzle.

But keep in mind the purpose of this chapter: God
wants us to trust Him today just as these great men and
women trusted Him in the past. Times have changed, but
God has not changed; and God still works in response to
faith. Let's trace some of these achievements and see how
they apply to our lives and ministries today.

Conquered kingdoms. Here we enter the realm of
national and international affairs. During the period of
the Judges, at least six different nations invaded the land
and put the people of Israel under bondage; yet God
raised up leaders who, by faith, attacked the enemy and
delivered the people. Gideon defeated the Midianites
(Judges 6—8). Barak joined with Deborah to overcome
the Canaanites led by Jabin (Judges 4, 5). Jephthah routed
the Ammonites (Judges 11, 12), and Samson made havoc
of the Philistines (Judges 12—16).

The Judges were not the only ones who "conquered
kingdoms." Both the kings and the prophets exercised
tremendous power as they listened for God's Word,
trusted God's power, and dared to face the enemy coura-
geously. King David defeated nation after nation in the
name of the Lord (see 2 Samuel 8); and Samuel, by his
prayers and his spiritual wisdom, helped the people to
victory. The word of prophets such as Elijah and Elisha
brought armies to defeat and rulers to ruin.

Does faith still operate in this realm today? Yes, it does.
Daniel 10:11-17 states that believing prayer affects the
nations, and that Satan and his angels oppose those who
pray in this way. When the early church confronted
opposition by those in power, they turned to God in

prayer and He answered (Acts 4:23ff.). One of the greatest needs today is for God's people to unite in believing prayer for world leaders (1 Timothy 2:1-4).

But there are also "personal kingdoms" that need to be conquered. "He who is slow to anger is better than the mighty, and he who rules his spirit, than he who captures a city" (Proverbs 16:32). "Like a city that is broken into and without walls is a man who has no control over his spirit" (Proverbs 25:28). It was said of Alexander the Great that he conquered the world but he could not conquer himself.

Self-control is one of the fruits of the Spirit, and this fruit prospers in an atmosphere of faith. As we yield ourselves to the Lord and believe His Word, His Spirit enables us to conquer the "kingdom within us" and to practice self-control. David won many victories in his lifetime, but one of the greatest was when he refused to retaliate against King Saul when he had the opportunity. There is room for that kind of victory in the Church today.

Performed acts of righteousness. Any act that is done in the name of the Lord, by faith, for His glory, is an act of righteousness. When Elijah challenged the prophets of Baal and defeated them, it was an act of righteousness. When Elisha healed Naaman, it was also an act of righteousness. The prophets who preached the Word, as well as the warriors who wielded the sword, were all serving God and seeking to bring about righteousness in the land.

The believing leaders that God raised up sought to rule the people under the righteous hand of God. "So David reigned over all Israel; and David administered justice and righteousness for all his people" (2 Samuel 8:15). Certainly it is God's desire that righteousness and justice prosper in the land. Joseph in Egypt ruled in righteousness, as did Esther in Persia and Daniel in Babylon. God still needs believing people who will accept places of authority and use their offices to promote righteousness and justice.

Obtained promises. We must be careful to distinguish

between "promises" and "the promise." Hebrews 11:39 makes it clear that none of these men and women of faith obtained *the promise*, that is, to meet the promised Savior in His day of ministry. They saw Him afar off (11:13) but they did not have the privilege of meeting Him in person and witnessing His ministry. "For truly I say to you, that many prophets and righteous men desired to see what you see, and did not see it; and to hear what you hear, and did not hear it" (Matthew 13:17).

But they did receive promises from the Lord, and by believing these promises, they accomplished God's will. Whenever they faced an impossible situation, God gave them a promise to believe; and when they believed God, He went to work on their behalf. "Not one of the good promises which the Lord had made to the house of Israel failed; all came to pass" (Joshua 21:45). "Blessed be the Lord, who has given rest to His people Israel, according to all that He promised; not one word has failed of all His good promise, which He promised through Moses His servant" (1 Kings 8:56).

Christians who live in God's Word, who read it systematically, who meditate on it and seek to obey it, always have a special message from God just when they need it. There is always a promise from the heart of God to sustain us in the difficult hours. Sometimes we find that promise in our daily reading of the Word. Other times we are reminded of some promise by the indwelling Holy Spirit, or another Christian may feel led of God to share a promise with us.

We have a Bible filled with promises! And these men and women of faith suffered, and even died, so that we might have the sure promises of God!

Shut the mouths of lions. Both David and Samson killed lions (Judges 14:5, 6; 1 Samuel 17:34), but the reference here is surely to Daniel's experience recorded in chapter 6 of his prophecy. For one thing, Daniel faced lions—plural—while the other men fought single beasts;

and Daniel testified, "My God sent His angel and shut the lions' mouths" (Daniel 6:22). The lions were not slain; they were rendered incapable of hurting God's servant.

We will never know until we get to heaven just how much God's angels have done for us (Hebrews 1:14). Certainly God's armies have protected us in ways that are hidden from us today. When the servant of God is doing the will of God, he must have faith that the angels of God will guide and guard him. The Christian who "abides in the shadow of the Almighty" can claim the protecting promises found in Psalm 91: "For He will give His angels charge concerning you, to guard you in all your ways" (v. 11).

Quenched the power of fire. The reference is to the three courageous Hebrews of Daniel chapter 3. They knew it was wrong to bow before idols; so, by faith, they refused to submit. They did not know for sure that God would deliver them; but, even if He did not, they still were not going to worship a heathen idol! Their faith did not extinguish the fire; it made the fire harmless. In fact, their clothing didn't even smell!

God does not promise to keep us out of the fire, but He does promise to go with us into the fire and to care for us. "When you pass through the waters, I will be with you; and through the rivers, they will not overflow you. When you walk through the fire, you will not be scorched, nor will the flame burn you" (Isaiah 43:2). This promise is not an invitation to tempt God and do foolish things, but it is an assurance we can cling to when we are in the will of God in the midst of danger.

Escaped the edge of the sword. Satan is a murderer and a destroyer. Ever since Cain killed Abel, Satan and his hosts have been seeking to destroy the servants of God. No sooner was Israel delivered from Egypt than the Amalekites attacked them. But Moses interceded on the mountain and Israel escaped the sword (Exodus 17:8-16).

David was rescued many times from enemy swords (Psalm 144:10). Jeremiah's life was threatened many times, yet God delivered him.

Hebrews 11:37 makes it clear that it is not always God's will that believers be delivered. We will discuss this when we study verses 36-40.

From weakness were made strong, became mighty in war, put foreign armies to flight. These phrases go together as they describe the warfare of faith. We make the mistake of thinking that the great men and women of faith were somehow *essentially* different from us, but they were not. "All God's giants have been weak men," said J. Hudson Taylor, "who did great things for God because they reckoned on His being with them." The difference is *faith*. "Want of trust is at the root of almost all our sins and all our weaknesses," said Hudson Taylor.

Apart from the power of God, Samson was as weak as any other man. Gideon was a trembling farmer, hiding in a winepress, when God called him; yet his faith in God made him a conqueror. Barak begged Deborah to assist him in the battle, and out of his fear and weakness God gave strength and victory. Jephthah was the rejected son of a prostitute, yet God used him to win a mighty victory. God did not *substitute* strength for their weakness; *out of* their weakness, He made them strong. "For when I am weak, then I am strong" (2 Corinthians 12:10).

God made these believers "mighty *in* war" [italics mine], not mighty *before* the war. They had the faith to get into the battle; and in the midst of the fight, they were strengthened by God. He gave them the power of His Spirit. "So the Spirit of the Lord came upon Gideon" (Judges 6:34). "Now the Spirit of the Lord came upon Jephthah" (Judges 11:29). Three times we are told that the Spirit of the Lord came upon Samson "mightily" (Judges 14:6, 19; 15:14). "But you shall receive power when the Holy Spirit has come upon you . . ." (Acts 1:8).

When these soldiers of faith "put foreign armies to flight," they were helping their people regain lost territory that had been captured by the enemy. How much "captured territory" the Church needs to reclaim! And we can do it only by faith.

Women received back their dead by resurrection. Death is the ultimate enemy, so resurrection is the ultimate victory. The reference here is to Elijah raising the widow's son (1 Kings 17:17-24) and Elisha raising the son of the Shunammite woman (2 Kings 4:8ff.). The fact that Jesus raised the dead was an indication of His messiahship (Matthew 11:1-6). The ability to perform such wonders was also a mark of a true apostle (Hebrews 2:3, 4; Romans 15:18, 19). There is no indication from Scripture that we can claim such signs today.

However, the "power of His resurrection" is available to us today (Philippians 3:10). "Now to Him who is able to do exceeding abundantly beyond all that we ask or think, according to the power that works within us" (Ephesians 3:20). Note where his resurrection power works: "within us"—God's people! By faith, we can experience resurrection power and see God do great things in us and through us. Like Abraham and Sarah, we may consider ourselves (or our ministries) "as good as dead" (Romans 4:19), and yet see God's resurrection power transform us (and our ministries) to the glory of God.

In the exercise of faith, God uses a variety of people, and these people solve a variety of problems. This leads us to a third lesson:

3. FAITH RELEASES A VARIETY OF POSSIBILITIES.
Unbelief will always lock up our potential, but faith will release it. There is tremendous potential in every Christian, but it can be released only by faith.

David was a teenage shepherd who became a great warrior and a great king. What made the difference? *Faith in God.*

Gideon was a frightened farmer who knew nothing

about fighting wars, yet he became a victorious general. What did it? *Faith in God.*

Jephthah, the son of a harlot, was rejected by his family and neglected by his nation; yet God used him to bring a great deliverance in Israel. What was the secret? *Faith in God.*

Moses appeared to be a failure at first, but God transformed him into a successful leader who built a mighty nation. What made him change? *Faith in God.*

The eyes of unbelief look at these "winners" listed in Hebrews 11, and the response is, "We can't understand it! These people have nothing special that they can claim, and yet they accomplished marvelous things! What was their secret?" *Faith in God.*

God has not changed.

The challenge has not changed.

We have changed. We no longer really believe in God. The God of Abraham, Gideon, Elijah, and David still lives—but where are the Abrahams, Gideons, Elijahs, and Davids who will trust Him?

"Time will fail me" wrote the author—but there is still time for more great deeds of faith, and there is still room to add your name to this list!

There are untapped resources in your life just waiting to be released, if you will only yield to God and trust His Word.

God has not changed, and He can still change you . . . and through you, change your world.

11/ THE OTHER SIDE OF FAITH
HEBREWS 11:35b—40

"God did it for me, and I know He will do it for you!"

Have you ever heard those words from a preacher or another believer bearing witness? Have you ever read them in a book? *They are dangerous words!* They give the impression that God *always* works the same way, in similar or identical situations. "If God healed me," says the enthusiastic witness, "He will also heal you! Now, all you have to do is—" and there follows the sure-fire "formula" for experiencing God's healing.

I received a phone call from a frantic young lady who kept shouting, "It doesn't work! It doesn't work!"

"What doesn't work?" I asked, after she had calmed down.

"I did everything they told me to do at the seminar, I followed all the steps, *and it doesn't work!*" She was so distraught that she threatened to commit suicide.

Doctors warn us that it's dangerous to take medicine that is prescribed for someone else, and that same warning can be applied to the spiritual life. We should beware of comparing our spiritual experiences with those of others. God's principles are always the same for every

believer, but His plans and purposes may be different.
God always honors faith, but we who believe must permit
Him to honor it in His own way. The Apostles James and
Peter both had great faith in God; yet James was slain and
Peter was miraculously delivered from prison (Acts 12).

At the word "others" in verse 35, we reach an important
turning point in Hebrews 11. The writer now lists some
"winners" who appeared to be losers! *They suffered and
did not experience miraculous escapes.* Did God fail
them? Did they fail God? The answer to both questions is
an emphatic no! These unnamed heroes of faith glorified
God just as much as the ones named in the first thirty
verses of the chapter. The one group glorified God in
their *escaping,* while the other glorified God in their
enduring.

It is for this reason that we must not practice "formula
faith" and "carbon copy Christianity." All believers in
every church must work out their own salvation (Philippians 2:12, 13) because each believer and each church is
unique in the plan of God. God is sovereign in His deal-
ings with His people, and we must recognize and respect
that sovereignty. Our faith must be like that of Mary:
"Behold, the bondslave of the Lord; be it done to me
according to your word" (Luke 1:38).

1. THE LIFE OF FAITH IS COSTLY.
Certainly the people named in the first part of the chapter
paid a price to trust God. Abel, the first martyr, gave his
life. Abraham had to give up his home and family, and
Moses refused the treasures and pleasures of Egypt.
David was persecuted by Saul until the time came for
God to establish the kingdom. But in spite of these
sacrifices, these men and women of faith seemed almost
to live "charmed lives." God did wonderful things in and
for them, even providing miraculous escapes from death.

Now scan the closing verses of Hebrews 11 and note

the new vocabulary: tortured . . . mockings and scourg-
ings . . . chains and imprisonment . . . stoned . . . slain
with the sword . . . destitute, afflicted, ill-treated!
   Could God have delivered these dedicated saints?
Certainly, but that was not His plan. Was God being
unfair by helping one group escape the sword while
another group was slain by the sword? No, not in the
least. "The thing molded will not say to the molder, 'Why
did you make me like this,' will it?" (Romans 9:20). God's
plans and providences are not limited by our feeble
understanding or explanations. "Oh, the depth of the
riches both of the wisdom and knowledge of God! How
unsearchable are His judgments and unfathomable His
ways!" (Romans 11:33).
   Remember, faith is not believing in spite of evidence.
That's superstition. True faith is obeying in spite of circumstance *and consequence.* Like the three Hebrews, we
must say: "If it be so, our God whom we serve is able to
deliver us from the furnace of blazing fire . . . *but even if
He does not,* let it be known to you, O king, that we are
not going to serve your gods or worship the golden image
that you have set up" (Daniel 3:17, 18, italics mine).
   Yes, the life of faith is costly.
   Some were tortured. Had they recanted their faith, they
would have been released; but they would rather die for
their faith than deny their faith. Release was available—
the temptation was there; but they resisted it and laid
down their lives for their Lord. In so doing, they obtained
"a better resurrection." Better than what? Better than the
resurrection described in the first part of Hebrews 11:35.
For, after all, the women received their dead back to life,
and they died again. But when these martyrs are raised
from the dead, they will share the glory of Christ and
never suffer or die again!
   People who live by faith live for the future. They do not
sacrifice the permanent on the altar of the immediate.
They live "with eternity's values in view."

Some were mocked and scourged. This suggests official opposition by the authorities. After all, our Lord was mocked and scourged, and shall His followers escape? Mockery is an indication that we are not being taken seriously, or that the enemy is *afraid* to take us seriously. For the early church, it started at Pentecost: "But others were mocking and saying, 'They are full of sweet wine' " (Acts 2.13). Soon the mocking turned to threatening (Acts 4:21), and the threatening to flogging (Acts 5:40). Listen to Paul's witness: "Five times I received from the Jews thirty-nine lashes. Three times I was beaten with rods . . ." (2 Corinthians 11:24, 25).

Some were chained and imprisoned. Again, official opposition, not unlike that which is going on today in countries behind iron and bamboo curtains. Jesus promises a special reward for those who are concerned about prisoners (Matthew 25:36). "Remember the prisoners, as though in prison with them, and those who are ill-treated, since you yourselves also are in the body" (Hebrews 13:3).

Some were treated brutally. The modern emphasis on "human rights" often appears to be more rhetoric than reality. And in their time, these great men and women of faith were treated worse than animals. This was sometimes done *in the name of religion.* It was the false prophets who persecuted and killed the prophets of old, and it was the official religious council that crucified Jesus Christ and persecuted the Church. "They will make you outcasts from the synagogue," promised the Savior; "but an hour is coming for everyone who kills you to think that he is offering service to God" (John 16:2).

How many of God's faithful servants have been stoned by blind and ignorant people! According to Jewish tradition, the prophet Isaiah was sawn in two with a wooden saw. It would be impossible to list all the believers who were slain by the sword. Of course, today there are other means for taking a life, and in some parts of the world *right now*, they are being used to persecute and destroy God's people.

If they would deny the faith, they would receive a better life; but would they receive a better resurrection or a better reward?

Some were deprived of the necessities of life, such as food, clothing, and shelter. A brilliant Christian in Moscow spends his days sweeping the street. If he would abandon his faith, he would be given a university education and a government position. Instead of being treated like human beings, made in the image of God, these early saints were hounded and hunted like animals. Were they cowards for fleeing and hiding? Of course not! Read the book of Acts and note how Paul often kept just one step ahead of his enemies.

If these people had been dangerous criminals, we could understand why they were chased out of decent society and forced to hide in caves; but they were not criminals. They were the salt of the earth! Man's inhumanity to godly men and women is proof of the depravity of the human heart.

For the most part, the church in the western world is protected and almost pampered. But it may not always be so. "Beloved, do not be surprised at the fiery ordeal among you, which comes upon you for your testing, as though some strange thing were happening to you" (1 Peter 4:12). The pampered church may one day become a persecuted church, and then God will make it clear who the true men and women of faith are. The fire will try every professed Christian's testimony, and the day will declare those who are true and those who are false. The wheat will be separated from the chaff and the sheep from the goats.

Where will you stand?

Do you have a faith worth suffering for?

2. THE LIFE OF FAITH IS REWARDED.

From the human point of view, these suffering people were all failures. Had they not been such "fanatics" about their faith, they could have "amounted to something" in the world. How foolish they were to pay such a price and get so little in return!

Well, what did they get in return?

Cod made them men and women "of whom the world was not worthy." True, they were rejected by society. The "important people" of the world either laughed at them or persecuted them. While the unbelievers were living in luxury, these believers were struggling to stay alive. Yet they were such magnificent specimens of godly life and character that they were actually *too good* to remain in such a wicked world!

The world always learns too late who her real heroes are. Jesus excoriated the Pharisees because they built tombs for the prophets and decorated monuments for the righteous (Matthew 23:29-32). What was their sin? While they were building and decorating tombs and monuments, they were persecuting and killing people *just as worthy as the dead heroes they were honoring!* Alas, even the professing Church has not always recognized the prophets and wise men God has sent to awaken and purge her. Before the blood of the martyrs is the seed of the Church, it is sometimes the shame of the Church.

The approval of God means more than the praise of men. After all, this world system is passing away, and that includes *Who's Who*, the social register, and the annual surveys of the most popular people (1 John 2:15-17). "But the one who does the will of God abides forever!" Scores of Anglican ministers closed their doors to the preaching of John Wesley. The names of these men are, for the most part, forgotten; but the Church around the world gives thanks for the life and ministry of Wesley.

But God did something more than just approve them

and make them people of worth (Hebrews 11:39). *He gave them His witness.* This is one of the key ideas in this chapter (vv. 2, 4, 5). They received that inner witness from God that He accepted them and approved of them. This inner witness to faith enables the suffering believer to endure to the glory of God. Knowing that we are right before God gives us the strength to accept all that is wrong from men. Yes, this inner witness does more than enable us to endure: it enables us to triumph!

"You say God helps those who trust him," a heckler called to a street preacher. "What did God ever do for Stephen?"

Quickly the preacher replied, "He gave him the love to be able to pray for his murderers!"

Stephen's faith did not rescue him from stoning; in fact, it was the cause of his death. But his faith did give him a shining face and a radiant testimony to the very end (Acts 7:54-60). Only the grace of God can enable a man to pray, "Lord, do not hold this sin against them!" (v. 60).

These men and women who ran so successfully in the race of faith did not receive the promise in their lifetime. They knew that the Savior would come. They knew there would one day be a heavenly city, populated by the people of faith. All the patriarchs looked for that city, but they never entered it while on earth. They continued to live in temporary tents.

Moses kept his eyes on the eternal reward. He lived by looking at the invisible! Yet he never received that promise in his life.

But just think of what that promise meant to these heroes! It was their "blessed hope" that spurred them onward when their zeal flagged and the way seemed impossible. It was their "living hope" that energized them with spiritual power. Abraham looked *for* a city and kept his life clean for God's glory. Lot looked *at* a city (Sodom) and wasted his life. Abraham won the race; Lot became a casualty, disqualified from the race because he broke the rules.

Yes, the life of faith is costly; but the life of unbelief is far more costly. God rewards the life of faith, but He cannot reward disobedience and unbelief.

3. THE LIFE OF FAITH UNITES ALL BELIEVERS.

Why didn't God encourage His suffering people by giving them what was promised? *He was thinking about us today!* "Because God had provided something better for us. . . ."

"Something better" is a major theme of the book of Hebrews. Since his readers were tempted to go back into the empty husk of the Hebrew religion, the writer pointed out over and over that what Jesus Christ has to offer is *better.* Jesus Christ is better than the prophets (1:1-3), the angels (1:4—2:18), Moses (3:1—4:13) and Aaron (4:14—6:20). He has a superior priesthood because He belongs to the order of Melchizedek, not the order of Aaron.

The sacrifice that Jesus Christ offered is better because it is founded on a better covenant (ch. 8) and ministered in a better sanctuary (ch. 9). Jesus Christ shed His own blood for us. His sacrifice is better than that of animals, offered under the law (ch. 10).

Something better!

We have in Christ a better hope (7:19), based on better promises (8:6). We have a better substance in heaven (10:34) and a better country awaiting us (11:16).

Something better!

Had God fulfilled His promise in the Old Testament period, there would have been no New Testament period—and we would have been left out! We, today, have "something better" because we look back, by faith, to the completed redemption that Christ wrought on the cross. The Old Testament saints certainly had a valid spiritual experience, but it was imperfect. We, today, share in a perfect sacrifice (the word *perfect* is another key word in Hebrews) and enjoy a perfect standing before God. The Old Testament worthies in heaven now share in Christ's perfection in glory (Hebrews 12:23).

God's dispensations may change, but His principles remain the same from age to age. He always has His people, and His people are always saved by faith. Apart from us, these heroes could not be made perfect. The fullness of the times had to come.

But if we have privileges that they did not have (and our Lord suggests this in Matthew 13:16, 17), then this makes their faith even that much more wonderful! What an argument for the readers of this epistle to "press on to maturity" and "hold fast [their] confession" (Hebrews 6:1; 4:14).

All of the people mentioned in Hebrews 11 share, with us, in the life and blessing of faith. They encourage us to keep running the race with endurance. And they all point to the greatest Winner of them all, Jesus Christ, the Son of God.

12/ THE GREATEST WINNER OF ALL
HEBREWS 12:1–13

The Bible is a book of "therefores," because the Bible was written to be lived and not just to be learned. "But prove yourselves doers of the word, and not merely hearers who delude themselves" (James 1:22). Phillips Brooks said, "Christianity knows no truth which is not the child of love and the parent of duty." Duty that isn't based on doctrine didn't come from the heart of God, and doctrine that doesn't lead to duty certainly never will accomplish the will of God. Divine revelation must never be separated from human responsibility.

Christian living is simply our loving response to what God has already done for us. God doesn't say, "Now do this, and I will reciprocate and do something wonderful for you." Rather, He says, "See what I have already done for you! Now I want you to respond by being lovingly obedient to my will." The more we understand our marvelous position in Jesus Christ, and the better we appreciate the redemption He purchased for us, the greater should be our desire to please God and obey His will.

What was God's desire for the believers who received this letter? *That they keep on moving forward in their*

Christian life. "Let us press on to maturity" (Hebrews 6:1). The image he uses in this section is that of a runner in the Greek or Roman athletic contests. These contests were important to the citizens because each town wanted to capture glory for itself and honor for its district. Preparing for the races, obeying the rules, and bringing home a crown were of great importance to the contestants. They wanted to do their best and they wanted to win the prize.

"Let us run with endurance" is the exhortation that the writer gives. But how do you do that? Life wasn't easy for these early Christians. They were persecuted and arrested and had even been made spectacles before their friends and neighbors (10:32-39). It would have been so much easier to go back to Judaism and escape a great deal of suffering!

But it isn't necessary for *any* believer to go back to the old life! In these verses, the writer gives us a number of considerations that can encourage us to run the race successfully and not quit or go back.

1. CONSIDER THE WINNERS (Hebrews 12:1a).

The great "cloud of witnesses" is made up of the people mentioned in Hebrews 11, the ordinary men and women who won the race because they exercised faith in God. The word "witnesses" does not mean "spectators," as though these people are now watching us from heaven. We have already seen that this concept of "witness" is important to the life of faith; for when we are living by faith, God bears witness to us and gives us His approval (11:2, 4, 39). The great heroes of faith bear witness to us because God first bore witness to them.

Christians are supposed to encourage one another (10:25), and this includes the believers of past centuries. One of my delights is the reading of Christian biography. I have hundreds of volumes of biography and autobiography in my library, and I find that reading the lives of great Christians is an encouragement to my own spiritual life. Likewise, the accounts of "Bible greats" found in the Word of God ought to encourage us as we seek to win the race of faith.

The Bible is primarily a revelation about God, but that revelation comes through the lives of ordinary people such as Abraham, Jacob, Moses, Daniel, and Gideon. The New Testament adds Peter, John, Paul, Barnabas, and even a temporary failure such as John Mark! When you read the Bible with this in mind, the lives of these men and women cannot but strengthen your faith.

Consider just a few of the people mentioned in Hebrews 11, the "winners" that are witnessing to us today and assuring us that the race can be won.

Have you ever faced family opposition? Then get acquainted with Abel, who was killed by his brother, or with Joseph, who was sold by his brothers!

Moving to a new city and a new home can be a difficult experience, but Abraham did it—by faith!

If others have hurt you, remember Joseph. If anybody could have nursed a grudge and avenged himself, it was Joseph; yet he refused to retaliate. He forgave his brothers and even took care of them—by faith.

The next time you have to make a costly decision, remember Moses and the decisions he made—by faith. The treasures and pleasures of this world will mean very little to you, if you will let Moses encourage you.

So, when the race gets difficult and you feel like quitting, consider the winners, that great host of Bible personalities (Old Testament and New Testament) who have already run the race successfully. It can be done, even by ordinary people!

2. CONSIDER YOURSELF (Hebrews 12:1b).
When the race is difficult, we like to blame circumstances or other people, or even God. But it's possible that *we* are

the ones to blame! "Let us also lay aside every encumbrance, and the sin which so easily entangles us." With the exception of athletes involved in body-contact sports, the secret of success is to strip down to the essentials. Who ever heard of running the hundred-yard dash and carrying a fifty-pound sack of flour at the same time?

A few years ago, I began to have serious lower back problems. One day, I bent over in my office to pick up a piece of paper, and I couldn't straighten up! The pain was unbearable. Somehow I managed to leave my office, get to my car, and drive to the doctor. I must confess that he had been trying for some time to get me to lose weight, so this was his opportunity.

"I'm having back trouble," I told him, wincing with pain.

"No," he replied, "you're not having back trouble. You're having *front* trouble!"

He was right: I was carrying too much weight in front. Since then, I've gotten rid of the excess baggage, and I feel better. No wonder the best athletes watch their weight: they want to do their best.

What did the writer mean by *encumbrances?* He was probably referring to anything that keeps us from successfully running the race of faith, anything that distracts us or divides our attention. It might in itself be a *good* thing, yet if it hinders us, it's dangerous and must be removed. The Greek and Roman athletes often trained with weights so that they would feel "free" when they laid them aside. Some of our modern-day baseball players do the same thing before they step up to bat. Weights for training are one thing, but permanent weight is something else.

Good things can encumber us, but evil things will entangle us. Unless we get rid of the sin in our lives, that sin will trip us up and make us stumble and fall before we reach the goal; and then we will lose the prize. Perhaps by "the sin," the writer means the sin of unbelief, because his emphasis has been on faith. Unbelief was the sin that tripped up Israel and robbed a whole generation of the joys of the Promised Land. Faith moves us forward but unbelief trips us up and then turns us backward.

It requires discipline to be a winning runner. "And everyone who competes in the games exercises self-control in all things" (1 Corinthians 9:25). The winners do more than choose between the good and the bad: they choose between the better and the best (see Philippians 1:9-11). "On the other hand, discipline yourself for the purpose of godliness" (1 Timothy 4:7).

When we start to pack for a move, we discover how much excess baggage we have accumulated since the last move! "Why are we saving this?" is the big question. So, we advertise a garage sale, or we donate the "best junk" to some service organization, or perhaps just throw it all away! It's an expensive thing to move, and extra "junk" only adds to that expense; so why take it along?

Life is too short and the race is too difficult for us to carry weights we don't need. We must not be satisfied just to get rid of the sins that entangle us; we must also "peel off" the weight that encumbers us. When we do, we will discover the joy of running the race with freedom and success.

3. CONSIDER THE RACE ITSELF (Hebrews 12:1c).

What race should we run? "The race that is set before us."

Each runner was assigned a lane on the race track, and he was expected to stay in that lane. Paul had this same image in mind when he wrote Philippians 3:12-16. *We cannot run somebody else's race.* God has equipped us for our race; He has assigned a lane to each of us. And He will give us our own rewards when we reach our goals.

There is no competition in the Christian race of faith. We are competing *only with ourselves.* If we take our eyes off the goal, if we start to watch the other runners, we are bound to stray from our lane and create problems for the other racers. It isn't our responsibility to judge the performance of others. In the race of faith, you and I are not the judges: we are the runners!

An incident from the life of Peter illustrates this truth. After Peter had been restored to discipleship, Jesus said to him, "Follow Me!" Peter began to follow the Lord, but then he heard someone walking behind him; so he turned to see who it was. It was the Apostle John.

"Lord, and what about this man?" Peter asked.

"If I want him to remain until I come," replied Jesus, "what is that to you? You follow Me!" (John 21:19-22).

In my own ministry, when I've been prone to watch the other runners and perhaps be critical of them, the Lord's words have come to my mind: "What is that to you—follow Me!" We must run in our own lanes and keep our eyes of faith on our goals, not somebody else's! Often, when I have found the race demanding and difficult, it's been because of my own disobedience. I have gotten out of my own lane, trying to run somebody else's race!

4. CONSIDER THE LORD JESUS CHRIST
(Hebrews 12:2, 3).

The Christian life begins when the sinner "looks to Jesus Christ" by faith. "Look unto me, and be ye saved, all the ends of the earth: for I am God, and there is none else" (Isaiah 45:22, KJV). Sin came into the world because of a look ("When the woman *saw* that the tree was good for food . . ."—Genesis 3:6), and sin can be forgiven only when we look by faith to the Savior.

The Christian life will end with a look: "We know that, when He appears, we shall be like Him, because we shall see Him just as He is" (1 John 3:2). Then we will enter into glory!

But between these two experiences, we must live the life of faith and run the race of faith by "fixing our eyes on Jesus." We are saved by a single *act* of faith, but we are

sanctified by an *attitude* of faith. The Greek verb says
"constantly be looking away to Jesus and concentrating
on Him."

Jesus Christ is the greatest "winner" of them all! We
sometimes have the idea that, because He is God, it was
relatively easy for Him to run the race and finish His
work; but it was not. He lived His life on earth the same
way you and I must live: by faith in the Word of God.
From the beginning, Satan tempted our Lord to use His
divine powers to meet His needs; but He refused to yield.
"Although He was a Son, He learned obedience from the
things which He suffered" (Hebrews 5:8). The same
resources that were available to Him are available to us
today, and they still work. We have the power of the
Spirit, the Word of God, and faith.

We can "run with endurance the race that is set before
us" because "the Pioneer and Perfecter of faith" has
endured before us and can enable us to endure. *And He
endured so much more than we shall ever endure!* When
He was here on earth, our Lord experienced every kind of
trial and testing that a human can face, and He came
through victoriously. He is now seated at the right hand
of the Father's throne, and from that throne He can give
us all that we need to win the race. Because He is "the
Pioneer" of our faith, He can start us on the race and
open the way for us. Because He is "the Perfecter" of our
faith, He can enable us to finish the race and accomplish
His will. From start to finish, it is Jesus Christ who enables us to run with believing confidence and joyful
endurance.

Remember that men and women of faith have eyes that
look beyond the immediate problems and trials. Abraham
looked beyond and saw the heavenly city. Joseph looked
beyond and saw the victorious exodus of Israel from
Egypt. Moses endured because he looked beyond the
treasures of Egypt and saw the eternal reward. Jesus
Christ looked beyond the Cross to "the joy set before

Him." This is not to deny that there was joy in His obedience on the Cross, because we know that our Lord delighted to do the will of His Father. But it was His faith in the Father's promise—the glory *beyond* the Cross—that enabled Him to endure.

What was "the joy set before Him"?

The answer, or part of it, may be in Jude 24: "Now to Him who is able to keep you from stumbling, and to make you stand in the presence of His glory blameless with great joy."

It was the joy of presenting us, His bride, to the Father in glory! "Father, I desire that they also, whom Thou hast given Me, be with Me where I am, in order that they may behold My glory, which Thou hast given Me . . ." (John 17:24).

"Consider Him!" said the writer. "Fix your eyes on Him!" How do we do this? *Through the Word of God.* "And though you have not seen Him [as did the apostles], you love Him, and though you do not see Him now [with physical eyes], but believe in Him, you greatly rejoice with joy inexpressible and full of glory" (1 Peter 1:8).

If we want to endure, we must do what Moses did: "for he endured, as seeing Him who is unseen" (11:27). Through the eyes of faith, enlightened by the Word, we see the resurrected and enthroned Christ. He has finished His work! He has run the race successfully! He is able to make us "winners" as well!

The readers of this letter were being tempted to live by the visible, not the invisible. They could see the Jewish temple still standing in Jerusalem. Why talk about an invisible temple, a heavenly sanctuary that nobody could see? They could see (and smell) the sacrifices, and they could watch the high priest as he ministered at the altar. That was much easier to do than to believe in a High Priest in heaven, a Priest whose work was finished and who had no more sacrifices to offer.

Doubt begins with distraction, and distraction begins

when we start noticing the visible and neglecting the invisible. When doubt is cultivated too long, it turns into unbelief; and unbelief will trip us up and hinder us as we try to run the race of faith. Distraction creates doubt, and doubt creates discouragement, and discouragement can easily transform a runner into a quitter. "For consider Him who has endured such hostility by sinners against Himself, so that you may not grow weary and lose heart." By faith, look beyond the hostility to the joy that God has set before you, and it will keep you running the race.

The next time you are criticized, consider Him. They called Him a glutton, a drunkard, and even a deceiver!

The next time people fail you, consider Him. One of His closest associates betrayed Him, His chief-of-staff denied Him, and all of His intimate friends forsook Him!

The next time the pain seems unbearable, consider Him. He died on a cross.

The next time your work seems a failure, consider Him. Even some of His disciples thought He had failed!

Jesus Christ is our pattern for life and service (Philippians 2:1-11). He shows us that we must be servants if we would be rulers, that the suffering comes before the glory, the Cross before the crown. And He also shows us that we live by faith.

5. CONSIDER GOD'S DISCIPLINE (Hebrews 12:4-13). The word translated "discipline" ("chastening" in the KJV) does not necessarily mean "punishment." It simply means "the training of a child." At about the age of seven, Greek boys were enrolled in their local gymnasia where they were trained for manhood. This meant exercise, participation in the games, and the development of mind, spirit, and body. They were being prepared for maturity.

God wants to keep us *going* and keep us *growing*. "Let us press on to maturity" (Hebrews 6:1). He disciplines us because He loves us! (See Proverbs 3:11, 12.) The Father wants all of His precious children to reach their full potential, and this can be done only as they struggle with the trials and demands of life. The key word in this section is "son," which means "a mature son." God addresses us "as sons" and not as little children. The word *son* is used at least six times in this passage, emphasizing the key idea of maturity.

Athletes must discipline themselves if they ever hope to be winners. They must obey the training rules and submit to the plans of their coaches and trainers. But the results are worth it! "All discipline for the moment seems not to be joyful, but sorrowful; yet to those who have been trained by it, afterwards it yields the peaceful fruit of righteousness" (Hebrews 12:11).

Afterwards!

That means *faith*—waiting for God to accomplish His purposes!

Joseph didn't enjoy those years in prison; but *afterwards* he rejoiced in what God accomplished for him and in him.

Moses didn't enjoy the struggles he had with Pharaoh in Egypt; but *afterwards* he saw God's handiwork in mighty power, and it was worth it all.

David didn't enjoy those years of exile, when Saul treated him like a criminal; but *afterwards* he was able to praise God for what He had done in his life.

And one day we will be able to praise God—so we must not give up! One of the secrets of endurance in the race of faith is reminding ourselves that athletes must experience discipline, and that afterwards, it is worth every bit of the price that we pay.

The enemy (who always watches our race) wants us to believe that we are suffering because God doesn't love us; but just the opposite is true. "For those whom the Lord loves He disciplines" (12:6). He keeps us going and growing by keeping us knowing that His discipline is given in love. He also wants us to know that He understands just how much we can take, so we don't have to be afraid. "He disciplines us for our good, that we may share His holiness" (12:10). Sometimes the Father has to "spank" us when we break the training rules, but even that "spanking" is an evidence of His love and a tool of His holiness.

We must not treat His disciplines lightly (12:5) or fight against them (12:9). Rather, we must yield to them and let Him have His way. His disciplines encourage us to exercise our "spiritual muscles," and that helps us to grow.

Only a wise Father such as we have could figure out a way to make trials and sufferings work *for* us and not *against* us!

Whenever we find ourselves losing ground in the race of faith, we should take inventory of our spiritual lives.

Consider the winners and let them encourage us from their experiences recorded in the Word.

Consider ourselves, and see if there are encumbrances or entanglements that are making our progress difficult.

Consider the race and make sure we are in our own lane, running our own race and not another's.

Consider Jesus Christ and fix our eyes of faith on Him, because He is the greatest "winner" of all!

Finally, consider God's discipline, and don't faint under it. Strong muscles come from great challenges, and our Father knows how much we can endure.

"Let us run with endurance the race that is set before us!"

Books by Warren W. Wiersbe

In Praise of Plodders
Plodders are those who labor with determination and drive—whether pastor, teacher, choir director, or counselor. Drawing on years of ministry experience, Dr. Wiersbe offers sound advice and workable solutions to problems encountered by those who minister.
ISBN 0-8254-4048-3   144 pp.   paperback

Treasury of the World's Great Sermons
These 122 outstanding sermons are presented from 122 of the greatest preachers. A short biographical sketch of every preacher is also included. Complete with an index of texts and of sermons.
ISBN 0-8254-4002-5   672 pp.   paperback

Kregel Classic Sermons Series

Classic Sermons on the Attributes of God
ISBN 0-8254-4038-6   160 pp.   paperback

Classic Sermons on the Birth of Christ
ISBN 0-8254-4044-0   160 pp.   paperback

Classic Sermons on Christian Service
ISBN 0-8254-4041-6   160 pp.   paperback

Classic Sermons on the Cross of Christ
ISBN 0-8254-4040-8   160 pp.   paperback

Classic Sermons on Faith and Doubt
ISBN 0-8254-4028-9   160 pp.   paperback

Classic Sermons on Family and Home
ISBN 0-8254-4054-8   160 pp.   paperback

Classic Sermons on Heaven and Hell
ISBN 0-8254-3995-7   160 pp.   paperback

Classic Sermons on Hope
ISBN 0-8254-4045-9   160 pp.   paperback

Classic Sermons on the Names of God
ISBN 0-8254-4052-1   160 pp.   paperback

Classic Sermons on Overcoming Fear
ISBN 0-8254-4043-2   160 pp.   paperback

Classic Sermons on Praise
ISBN 0-8254-3994-9   160 pp.   paperback

Classic Sermons on Prayer
ISBN 0-8254-4029-7 160 pp. paperback

Classic Sermons on the Prodigal Son
ISBN 0-8254-4039-4 160 pp. paperback

Classic Sermons on the Resurrection of Christ
ISBN 0-8254-4042-4 160 pp. paperback

Classic Sermons on the Second Coming and Other Prophetic Themes
ISBN 0-8254-4051-3 160 pp. paperback

Classic Sermons on the Sovereignty of God
ISBN 0-8254-4055-6 160 pp. paperback

Classic Sermons on Spiritual Warfare
ISBN 0-8254-4049-1 160 pp. paperback

Classic Sermons on Suffering
ISBN 0-8254-4027-0 204 pp. paperback

Classic Sermons on Worship
ISBN 0-8254-4037-8 160 pp. paperback